The Windfall Instinct

The Psychology Behind Why Sudden Money Disappears So Fast

Jordan Ellis

First edition, 2026

Published by Jordan Ellis

This book is intended for general educational and reflective purposes only. It is not a substitute for professional financial, legal, medical, or mental health advice, diagnosis, or treatment. Always seek the advice of a qualified professional with any questions regarding your specific circumstances. Never disregard professional advice or delay seeking it because of something you have read in this book. Names and identifying details in any illustrative examples are anonymous/archetypal composites, not depictions of a single real individual.

Contents

Introduction

Picture the moment the number changes. A check arrives, or a deposit lands, or a lawyer's letter confirms what you'd stopped letting yourself hope for, and for a second the account balance on your phone looks unfamiliar, like a stranger's name attached to your face. You worked for some of the money you'll ever hold in your life. This isn't that money. This came from somewhere else — an inheritance, a bonus, a refund, a settlement, a gift, a stroke of luck — and it arrived without the thousand small Tuesdays that usually stand between you and a dollar. That absence is not a minor detail. It is the entire subject of this book.

Here is the pattern, stated plainly, before a single chapter tries to earn it: money that arrives without sustained personal effort gets treated by your mind as less real than money you worked for, and less-real money gets spent faster, looser, and with less resistance — regardless of the actual number on the check. A ten-thousand-dollar bonus and a ten-thousand-dollar year of overtime are, on a bank statement, identical. In your nervous system, they are not remotely the same event. One gets defended like a resource. The other gets treated like a temporary visitor you're already unconsciously planning to see off. This isn't a story about impulsive people or poor discipline. It happens to careful, responsible, financially literate people just as reliably as anyone else, because the mechanism doing it isn't a character flaw. It's a feature of how your mind sorts money by its story of origin, and windfalls get sorted into the one category your judgment guards least carefully.

You may already sense this in your own history, even if you've never had language for it. Think of the last time money arrived that you didn't have to earn through the ordinary grind of a paycheck. Maybe it was a tax refund that felt, for a few days, like a small piece of found treasure rather than what it actually was — your own money, withheld and returned, no different from a paycheck that arrived twelve months late. Maybe it was a wedding gift, a graduation check, an unexpected reimbursement, a settlement that closed out a long and exhausting dispute. However it arrived, notice how it left. Windfall money has a way of vanishing into small, forgettable purchases and a handful of larger ones you can barely reconstruct a year later, while the equivalent sum, had it come from four extra months of ordinary paychecks, would likely still show some trace of itself in your life — in a slightly higher savings balance, in a debt paid down, in something you could point to and say, that's where it went. Windfalls rarely leave that kind of trail. They tend to leave only the memory of having had them, and the faint, familiar bewilderment of not quite knowing where they went.

This book gives that bewilderment a name and, more importantly, a mechanism. Researchers who study decision-making under gains and losses have a term for what happens to your risk tolerance and your spending discipline once you're playing with money you feel you didn't fully earn: the house money effect, first named and studied by the economist Richard Thaler, drawing on the language of casino gamblers who treat their winnings differently than the money they walked in with. A gambler who arrives with two hundred dollars and leaves the table with five hundred will often gamble far more freely with the extra three hundred than they ever gambled with their original stake — not because the three hundred is worth less, but because it feels like the house's money, not theirs, even though the moment it entered their pocket, it became exactly as real, exactly as spendable, exactly as theirs as anything else in their wallet. The insight generalizes far beyond casinos. Any money that arrives without the felt weight of having been earned gets a version of this same discount applied to it, silently, by a part of your mind that was never consulted and never asked to explain itself.

It helps to understand what this book means, specifically, by "effort," since the word could be misread as narrower than it actually is. This isn't only about physical labor or the number of hours logged at a desk. Effort, in the sense this book uses it, is anything that requires sustained, ongoing decision-making over time — the discipline of setting aside part of a paycheck month after month, the patience of building a skill across years before it becomes billable, the persistence of showing up to a difficult job on the days you'd rather not. What all of these share is duration and repeated choice: you had to decide, over and over, to keep going, and each of those decisions left a small psychic mark that accumulates into something your mind recognizes as genuinely, durably yours. A windfall, whatever its size, skips that accumulation. It arrives as a single event rather than as the sum of many small, effortful choices, and that structural difference — one decision versus thousands — turns out to matter enormously to how protectively your mind treats the result.

This also means the house money effect isn't really about fairness, luck, or merit, even though those words tend to hover around any conversation about unearned money. Whether a windfall was deserved, lucky, generous, or overdue has almost no bearing on how the mechanism operates — an inheritance from a beloved parent and a lucky lottery ticket bought on a whim get filed under strikingly similar psychological rules, despite occupying entirely different moral categories in how most people would describe them. The mechanism doesn't consult your sense of whether you deserve the money. It only tracks whether the money arrived through the kind of sustained, repeated effort that leaves a psychic mark — and neither inheritance nor luck does, regardless of how differently we might otherwise think about them.

This is worth being precise about, because it would be easy to confuse this book with two other, related ideas, and confusing them would blur the exact thing this book is trying to sharpen. This is not a book about lifestyle creep — the slow, incremental expansion of spending that tracks a rising, earned income, where each raise quietly recalibrates what feels "normal" to spend until yesterday's luxury is today's baseline. Creep is gradual, and it happens to money you worked steadily for. This book is about the opposite shape: sudden money, spent suddenly, precisely because it never had to be worked for at all. And this is also not a book about mental accounting in the broader sense — the way your mind sorts money into labeled envelopes, treating a "vacation fund" differently than a "bills" fund even though both are the same dollars in the same account. That labeling matters, and it's a real pattern, but it's a story about categories. This book is about something narrower and, in a specific way, more elemental: not how money gets labeled once it's in your possession, but how the very fact of its arrival — earned, sweat-priced, invoiced, versus given, found, won, inherited — changes how real it feels before you've labeled it as anything at all. Two piles of identically labeled "savings" can still feel different if one came from a decade of paychecks and the other came from a phone call informing you of an inheritance. The source itself is doing work no label can fully capture.

Why does this distinction matter enough to build an entire book around it? Because windfalls are not rare events confined to lottery winners and heirs to fortunes. Nearly everyone reading this page will, at some point — has, at some point — held money that arrived without the felt cost of earning it. A holiday bonus. A refund from the government. A settlement from an accident or a dispute. A gift from a parent or a grandparent. An inheritance, large or modest, arriving at the worst possible moment, tangled up with grief. A stock grant or equity payout that turned, almost overnight, into a number larger than a year of salary. Money found in an old account, an unclaimed-property search, a security deposit you'd written off. None of these events are exotic. They are ordinary punctuation marks in an ordinary financial life, and every single one of them puts you, briefly, in the exact psychological position of the gambler holding the house's money — flush, untethered, and quietly primed to treat this pile differently than you'd treat the pile you built one paycheck at a time.

Consider two people holding the same amount of money on the same afternoon, arriving from two different directions. The first has spent eighteen months putting aside a fixed amount from every paycheck, watching a savings goal climb by small, visible increments, feeling the specific ache of skipped nights out and secondhand furniture that got her there. The second receives, on a Tuesday, a check for the identical amount — an inheritance from an aunt she barely knew, arriving through a lawyer's office with a cover letter and a condolence card. Ask each of them, honestly, how protective they feel of that exact sum, and you will hear two different relationships to the same number of dollars. The first defends her total like a wall she built brick by brick, resistant to erosion, alert to anything that threatens it. The second experiences her total more like weather — present, real in the moment, but somehow not quite hers in the way the first woman's savings are hers. Same number. Different psychology entirely. That gap is not a personality difference between these two women. It is the house money effect, operating exactly as it operates in nearly everyone, and it is the gap this book exists to close.

None of this means windfalls are dangerous in some moralized sense, or that money you didn't sweat for is somehow tainted or less deserved. That framing would be its own kind of trap — a puritanical instinct that says only suffering makes money legitimate, which is neither true nor useful and which this book explicitly rejects. A bonus is not a moral test. An inheritance is not a character exam. The point isn't that you need to earn every dollar's right to exist in your account through personal struggle. The point is narrower and more practical: because your mind treats windfall money as less real by default, without your consent and usually without your awareness, you are likely to make decisions with that money that you would never make with equally sized earned income — and many of those decisions are ones you would actively choose differently if you could see the mechanism clearly enough to interrupt it. This book isn't asking you to feel guilty about a windfall. It's handing you the ability to decide, consciously, what happens to it, instead of letting an unexamined reflex decide for you.

It's also worth being honest about why this particular blind spot survives so well in people who are otherwise financially careful. Most financial discipline is built through repetition — you build a habit of checking your balance, of comparing prices, of pausing before a large purchase, and that habit strengthens the more often it's exercised under the same conditions. Windfalls, by their nature, break the conditions the habit was built under. They're irregular, unpredictable, and structurally different from the paycheck cycle your discipline was trained on, which means the very muscle that makes you careful with regular income often simply doesn't activate for a windfall — not because the muscle is weak, but because the windfall doesn't look, to your trained reflexes, like the kind of event that muscle exists to guard against. This is why so many genuinely disciplined people are blindsided by their own windfall spending: their discipline was never actually tested against this specific shape of event, and untested discipline, however real, doesn't automatically generalize to situations it's never encountered.

The chapters ahead each take one shape this pattern wears — the inheritance that vanishes inside eighteen months, the bonus treated as permission rather than as pay, the tax refund spent like a coupon rather than banked like income, the settlement that gets spent grieving instead of rebuilding, the gift that gets discounted the moment it's handed over, the equity payout that evaporates into a lifestyle nobody remembers choosing, the forgotten account that resurfaces and disappears again within the month, the lucky win that primes you to gamble with money that was never house money to begin with — and does the same five things to it, every time. Shows you the moment as it actually happens, in enough close, specific detail that you recognize yourself rather than a stranger. Names the real mechanism underneath, drawn from actual, citable research in behavioral economics and psychology, never invented for the sake of sounding authoritative. Counts what it actually costs — in dollars, and in the quieter currency of what you didn't get to keep or build. Hands you concrete ways to interrupt the pattern, ways that live in your own decision-making rather than in any specific app, account, or platform. And closes with a single sentence built to survive contact with your actual life, something you could say to a friend standing in the exact spot you once stood in.

You'll notice, reading through, that these chapters cover very different kinds of windfalls — an inheritance is nothing like a tax refund, which is nothing like a lawsuit settlement, which is nothing like a birthday check from a grandmother. That variety is deliberate. The house money effect doesn't care about the source's emotional weight or its legal category. It runs the same underlying discount on grief money as it runs on lucky money, on money tangled up with loss as readily as on money tangled up with celebration. Seeing the same mechanism recur across such different circumstances is, in a strange way, the most useful thing this book can show you, because it means you'll be able to recognize the pattern the next time it shows up in a form none of these specific chapters predicted — a form of windfall this book never got around to naming, arriving in a year none of us can see yet.

One honest caveat before the chapters begin. This book will not tell you what to do with your next windfall — not in the sense of a specific allocation, a percentage to save, an account to open, a product to buy. That kind of advice ages badly, depends entirely on your circumstances, and isn't the actual gap this book is built to close. What you'll get instead is something more durable: a felt sense, the next time unexpected money lands in your hands, of what your mind is quietly about to do with it before you've consciously decided anything at all — and a few extra seconds, stretched wide enough to fit one real choice inside them, before the reflex runs the whole show. That gap between the windfall landing and your reflex spending it is, for most people, close to zero. The entire task ahead is widening it.

If you've picked up this book because you're currently holding, or about to hold, a specific windfall — an inheritance still working its way through probate, a bonus you're expecting next quarter, a settlement your attorney says is close — you might be tempted to skip straight to the one chapter that matches your situation. That's a reasonable instinct, and each chapter is built to stand on its own. But there's a real advantage to reading the chapters that don't seem to apply to you as well, because the underlying mechanism, not the specific windfall category, is the actual subject of this book. Someone who reads only the chapter on inheritance will understand inheritance money considerably better. Someone who reads all nine chapters will understand something more durable: the shape of a pattern that will keep recurring across an entire financial life, in forms this book couldn't have anticipated, long after the specific windfall that sent them looking for this book has been spent, saved, or otherwise resolved.

It's also worth saying plainly who this book is not written for, because misapplied advice can do real harm. If you are currently in a genuine financial crisis — behind on essential bills, facing an eviction, unable to cover a medical need — and a windfall has just arrived that could solve that crisis, this book's caution about slowing down is not an instruction to delay addressing an actual emergency. Nothing here should be read as advice to sit on money you urgently need for survival while you contemplate the psychology of house money. The patterns in this book describe discretionary spending — money that could, with a clearer head, have gone toward a goal, a cushion, or a genuine priority, but instead dissolved into purchases the recipient can barely reconstruct months later. If your situation is more urgent than that, act on the urgency first. The reflection this book asks for is for the funds and decisions that remain once the actual fires are out.

Here is the master thesis, worth repeating until it needs no footnote: **money that didn't cost you effort to get doesn't feel like it costs you anything to lose — and that feeling is wrong every single time, because a dollar spent is a dollar spent, no matter how easily it arrived.** Everything from here is the specific, evidence-based case for why that feeling is a trick of your own mind rather than a fact about the money, and what to do instead once you can see the trick clearly.

Let's start with the casino floor where the whole idea was first noticed — and the far quieter rooms in ordinary life where the same thing happens every day, to people who have never once set foot near a card table.

Chapter 1 — The House Money Effect

A man sits down at a blackjack table with four hundred dollars he withdrew from an ATM an hour earlier, money he thought about on the drive over, money he'd mentally already subtracted from what he could spend on anything else this month. He plays carefully. He splits pairs conservatively, doubles down only when the odds clearly favor it, walks away from a losing streak before it can compound. This is his money, and he treats it accordingly — with the wary respect of someone who knows exactly what four hundred dollars costs to replace.

Three hours later, he's up six hundred dollars. And something in how he plays has changed, though he couldn't tell you when or how. He's doubling down on hunches now. He's staying in hands he would have folded at hour one. He tips the dealer more generously, buys a round for the strangers next to him, feels a looseness in his chest that wasn't there when this was his four hundred dollars on the table. By the time he leaves — down to two hundred dollars of his winnings, having given back most of what he was ahead — he doesn't feel the loss the way he would have felt losing his original stake. It doesn't sting the same. It was never quite real money to him in the first place. It was house money. And house money, it turns out, is money you can afford to lose, even though, mechanically, dollar for dollar, it was never any different from the four hundred he walked in defending so carefully.

This is the scene that gave the mechanism its name, and it's worth sitting with the scene itself before moving to what it explains, because the scene is stranger than it first appears. The six hundred dollars this man won is not, in any accounting sense, different from the four hundred he arrived with. It sits in the same pocket. It spends at the same tables. It's worth exactly a dollar per dollar, same as always. And yet his brain has quietly filed it under a completely different set of rules — rules that permit recklessness his original stake would never have been allowed. Nothing about the money changed. Everything about how he related to it changed, the instant it arrived without the felt cost of having earned it through his own steady effort.

Watch the same mechanism play out somewhere that has nothing to do with cards or casinos. A woman opens a retirement account statement she hasn't looked at in six months and finds it's grown considerably more than she expected, driven by a strong run in the broader market rather than by anything she did differently — she didn't contribute more, didn't change her allocation, didn't make any active decision at all. The account is simply worth more than her mental model of it accounted for. In the weeks that follow, without ever consciously connecting the two events, she finds herself saying yes to a handful of purchases she'd normally have deferred — a nicer version of something she needed anyway, a spontaneous weekend trip, a slightly-too-expensive gift for a friend's birthday. None of this spending touches the retirement account itself; it's entirely funded by her regular checking balance. But her sense of her own financial cushion has quietly expanded to include a gain she didn't work for and can't even fully explain, and that expanded sense of cushion is doing exactly what the blackjack winnings did for the man at the table: making money that was never actually "extra" feel available for looser treatment, purely because of how recently and how easily it seemed to appear.

What's actually happening

The economist Richard Thaler, whose work over several decades reshaped how the field of economics understands actual human financial behavior rather than the idealized, perfectly rational behavior classical economic models assumed, is the researcher most responsible for naming this pattern precisely: the house money effect. Drawing on both casino observation and controlled experiments, Thaler and his collaborator Eric Johnson found that people who have just experienced a gain become measurably more willing to take risks with money connected to that gain than they would be with an equivalent amount of money from an untethered source — even when the two sums are, by any rational measure, completely interchangeable. Once you're "up," the additional money gets mentally coded as the casino's money rather than your own, and that recoding changes your risk tolerance in real time, in ways you don't consciously choose and often don't notice happening.

What makes the finding durable, rather than a mere curiosity about gambling behavior, is how consistently it replicated once other researchers began testing it outside casino settings entirely — in controlled experiments involving hypothetical financial decisions, in studies of how people treat unexpected income more broadly, and in the everyday, informal observation that gave the effect its name well before economists got around to studying it formally. The phrase itself predates Thaler's research; gamblers had been calling this exact pattern "playing with house money" for generations, an intuitive folk observation about their own psychology that Thaler and his colleagues took seriously enough to actually test, and confirmed held up under rigorous scrutiny rather than dissolving as a mere superstition. That's part of why this book treats it as a load-bearing concept rather than a passing metaphor: it's one of the rare cases where a piece of folk wisdom about human behavior turned out to be exactly right once researchers looked closely.

The mechanism sits inside a broader idea Thaler spent his career mapping: mental accounting, the observation that human beings do not treat money as the single, perfectly fungible resource that economic theory assumes it to be. Instead, people sort money into separate mental categories, and money in one category gets governed by entirely different rules than an identical sum sitting in another. This book's angle sits inside that larger territory but focuses on one specific, underexamined corner of it: not how money gets labeled once it's already in your account — vacation fund versus bills fund, an idea explored elsewhere — but how the very *source* of the money, earned versus windfall, changes its perceived reality before any label ever gets attached to it. A windfall doesn't need a label to feel different. It feels different the moment it lands, purely because of where it came from, and that felt difference is the house money effect in its rawest form.

Why would a mind built for survival do this? The likely answer runs through something psychologists call psychic cost — the subjective, felt weight of what it took you to acquire something, distinct from its objective market value. Money that arrived through sustained, effortful labor carries the psychic imprint of everything that went into earning it: the hours, the fatigue, the trade-offs, the version of your Tuesday you gave up to have it. That imprint makes the money feel weighty, worth protecting, worth thinking twice before spending. Money that arrived without that imprint — a gift, a windfall, a stroke of luck — carries none of that weight. It feels, quite literally, lighter in the hand, even though it weighs exactly the same on a bank statement. Your mind isn't tracking the dollar amount when it decides how carefully to guard a sum of money. It's tracking the story of how the money got here, and windfalls come with a story that reads, to your reflexes, as *this one doesn't count the same.*

It's worth pausing on why this shortcut might have made sense at some point, even though it clearly misfires in a modern financial life built around bank accounts, paychecks, and windfalls that behave nothing like the resources a mind evolved to track. In an environment without stored, fungible currency, a genuine windfall — a large, unexpected catch, a stroke of fortune in foraging, a gift from another group — really was different from steady, effortful provisioning, in ways that mattered for survival. Windfalls in that environment were often perishable, shareable, and disconnected from the ongoing, planned labor of gathering and hunting; treating them with a different set of rules, including a greater willingness to share or consume them quickly, may well have made evolutionary sense in a world where food spoiled and stockpiling was often impossible anyway. The trouble is that modern money doesn't spoil, doesn't need to be shared to avoid waste, and is every bit as durable and useful whether it arrived through a windfall or a decade of paychecks. The old shortcut persists, misapplied to a resource that no longer behaves the way the shortcut assumes it does.

There's a second layer to this, and it explains why the effect doesn't fade quickly even in careful, financially literate people. The psychologists Daniel Kahneman and Amos Tversky, in the foundational work on prospect theory that reshaped the study of decision-making under uncertainty, demonstrated that people don't evaluate outcomes against some fixed, objective zero point — they evaluate them relative to a reference point, usually their recent status quo, and losses relative to that reference point feel roughly twice as painful as equivalent gains feel pleasurable. Here's where this interacts with windfalls in a subtle and important way: a windfall temporarily resets your reference point upward, almost instantly, in a way earned income never quite does. The moment the inheritance clears, the moment the bonus posts, your mind quietly recalibrates what "normal" feels like to include that new total — and against that freshly inflated reference point, spending down the windfall doesn't register as a true loss the way spending down your carefully built savings would. You're not losing something from a stable baseline. You're merely returning, in your own mind's accounting, to something closer to where you started — which makes the spending feel almost cost-free, right up until the money is actually gone and the old baseline turns out to have been the real one all along.

It's worth being honest about the limits of what this research actually establishes, since overclaiming would undercut the very credibility this book depends on. Thaler and Johnson's original work, and the decades of replication and extension that followed, demonstrate the house money effect reliably across gambling contexts and a range of controlled financial decision experiments — the pattern is genuinely robust, not a one-off finding. What the research doesn't claim is that every person experiences the effect identically, or that it operates with the same intensity across every kind of windfall this book covers; individual differences in financial anxiety, cultural background, and prior experience with money all likely modulate how strongly the pattern shows up in any specific person's life. This book applies the mechanism broadly because the pattern recurs so consistently across the very different scenarios in the chapters ahead, but it's worth holding the research itself with appropriate precision: it establishes a real, well-documented tendency, not an iron law that predicts every individual's behavior with certainty.

Take a woman in her late thirties who receives a year-end bonus roughly equal to two months of her regular salary — a genuinely large sum, one she'd have described, a year earlier, as life-changing if you'd asked her to imagine it in the abstract. She works in a demanding role, has a mortgage, has been meaning to build a real emergency fund for three years running. When the bonus posts, she has, for about eleven days, a specific and vivid plan: half toward the emergency fund, a smaller portion toward the high-interest card she's been chipping at, and a modest amount — genuinely modest, she tells herself, maybe eight percent — set aside for something fun, because she's worked hard and a bonus should feel like something. By day twelve, the modest eight percent has become a spontaneous long weekend booked with a friend, upgraded to a nicer hotel than either of them would normally choose, "since we're already spending on the trip." By day twenty, a piece of furniture she'd been eyeing for months — priced well above what she'd ever have approved from her regular paycheck — arrives at her apartment, purchased in an evening, justified by the thought that the bonus made it "basically free" relative to what it would have cost her to save for it the normal way. Six weeks after the deposit, she does the math she'd been avoiding and finds that the emergency fund got roughly a third of what she'd planned, the card got even less, and the rest — the majority of a sum she once would have called life-changing — is now distributed across a weekend, a piece of furniture, and a string of smaller purchases she genuinely cannot fully reconstruct. She is not a reckless person. She is, in every other domain of her financial life, careful, deliberate, someone who reads the fine print. The bonus simply arrived pre-coded, in her own mind, as house money — money that had already, before she'd spent a cent of it, been quietly filed under *this doesn't count the same as my salary.*

Why this book, and why now

This mechanism is the spine the rest of this book stands on, and every chapter ahead is an application of it to a different kind of windfall, because the house money effect doesn't discriminate by source. It runs on a casino floor and it runs identically on a kitchen table where a settlement check just arrived. It runs on a bonus and it runs on a tax refund, on a wedding gift and on a forgotten account that resurfaces after eleven years, on an equity payout that turned a software engineer's net worth upside down overnight and on the twenty-dollar bill found in an old jacket pocket. The dollar amounts differ enormously across these cases. The underlying psychology does not.

Chapter 2 looks at the inheritance — money tangled up with grief, arriving at exactly the moment a person is least equipped to make careful decisions, and disappearing with a speed that shocks the people who receive it more than anyone watching from outside. Chapter 3 looks at the bonus, and the way it gets mentally filed as a reward for enduring work rather than as pay for work performed, which changes what it feels permissible to do with it. Chapter 4 looks at the tax refund — genuinely your own money, withheld and returned, and yet treated by nearly everyone who receives one as found money rather than as the delayed paycheck it actually is. Chapter 5 looks at the lawsuit settlement, money that arrives carrying the specific psychic residue of an injury, a dispute, a loss, and how that residue changes spending behavior in ways that surprise the people living through it. Chapter 6 looks at the gift — money handed over by someone who loves you, and the strange way a gift's emotional context can make it feel even less "real" as money than a windfall with no emotional attachment at all. Chapter 7 looks at the equity payout, the sudden, often disorienting arrival of a sum that dwarfs years of ordinary salary, and the specific ways that scale changes the house money effect's grip. Chapter 8 looks at found or forgotten money — the resurfaced account, the unclaimed property, the security deposit you'd long since written off — and the particular vanishing act this smallest category of windfall performs. Chapter 9 looks at lottery-adjacent luck: not necessarily a jackpot, but any stroke of good fortune that primes a person to treat their entire financial life, briefly, the way the man at the blackjack table treated his six hundred dollars of winnings.

By the end, you'll have something most people never get: a name for the specific moment a windfall's story overrides your judgment about its size, and a handful of ways to interrupt that moment before it spends money you'll wish, eighteen months from now, you still had.

The overrides

Notice the recoding, out loud, the moment money arrives without effort attached. The instant you receive a windfall — a check, a deposit, a transfer, however it comes — say to yourself, plainly: *this is not house money. This is exactly as real as anything I've ever earned.* This sounds almost too simple to matter, and it is simple, but simplicity is the point. The house money effect operates below conscious language; naming it out loud, even briefly, pulls it up into a level of awareness where you can actually negotiate with it, rather than letting it run automatically in the background.

Rename the money by its function, not its origin, before you plan anything with it. Instead of thinking of it as "the bonus" or "the inheritance" or "the refund," think of it as what it actually is once it's sitting in your account: money. The same money that would be sitting there if it had arrived through eight months of ordinary paychecks instead. Ask yourself directly: if this exact sum had arrived as part of my regular income instead of as a windfall, what would I actually do with it? The honest answer is almost always more conservative than what the windfall framing was about to produce — and that gap is the bias itself, made visible enough to correct.

Build in a mandatory pause before any windfall decision, and make the pause a decision-process rule rather than a one-time promise. Give yourself a fixed window — long enough to let the initial spike of "found money" excitement fade, short enough that you're not just procrastinating — before making any discretionary decision about a windfall larger than a week's ordinary spending. During that window, do nothing with the money except let it sit, fully liquid, fully available, so you're not restricting your options — you're just declining to act on the first impulse the money produces.

Ask what your most careful self, not your most excited self, would do. Windfalls arrive during a spike of positive feeling, and decisions made during that spike are systematically different from decisions made once the spike has settled. Before committing to anything, picture the version of yourself who is calmest and most deliberate about money — the one who reads statements fully, who plans two steps ahead — and ask what that version of you would do with this exact sum. That's usually a more reliable guide than whatever the excited version of you wants to do in the first hour.

Track the background cushion effect, not just direct spending. As the retirement-statement example shows, a windfall doesn't have to be spent directly to loosen your discipline elsewhere — its mere existence can quietly expand your felt sense of financial safety and make unrelated, regular-income spending feel more permissible than it actually is. Periodically ask whether a recent gain, even one you haven't touched, might be making you feel more flush than your actual, ongoing cash flow supports.

If you're holding a windfall right now, run this exercise before reading any further. Write down, in one sentence, exactly what kind of windfall it is and roughly how large. Then write a second sentence: if this exact amount had arrived as ordinary income spread across the last several months instead, what would I have already done with it? Compare the two sentences honestly. The distance between them is the house money effect, made visible in your own handwriting rather than in someone else's story — and that visibility is worth more than any abstract description of the mechanism could be.

Rule to remember: *money doesn't know how it got to you, and it shouldn't get to decide how carelessly you treat it just because it arrived without a fight. Every dollar deserves the same defense, whether you earned it in a year or received it in an envelope.*

Chapter 2 — The Inheritance

Why Grief Money Disappears Faster Than Any Other Kind

She is standing in her mother's kitchen four days after the funeral, holding a checkbook that isn't hers, trying to remember whether she's eaten today. The lawyer's letter arrived the week before, spelling out numbers she hadn't let herself think about while her mother was still alive to be thought of instead — a modest but real inheritance, the accumulated result of a woman who clipped coupons for forty years and never once, in her daughter's memory, bought anything she didn't need. The daughter sits at the same kitchen table where she did homework as a child, and the number on the estate paperwork feels less like money and more like a message in a language she doesn't fully speak yet, one final thing her mother is trying to tell her that she isn't ready to hear.

The first few weeks pass in the fog everyone warns you about and nobody manages to actually prepare for. She goes back to work because staying home feels worse, and colleagues who know about the funeral treat her with a careful gentleness that somehow makes the whole thing feel less real rather than more. The estate paperwork sits on her kitchen counter, untouched, for nearly a month — not because she's avoiding it exactly, but because opening it means confronting, in black and white, the specific dollar figure her mother's entire life of careful frugality amounted to, and some part of her isn't ready to see her mother's decades reduced to a number on a page. When she finally does open it, the number is larger than she expected. Her mother, it turns out, had been quietly, methodically saving for longer and more successfully than anyone in the family had ever guessed, living modestly not out of necessity but out of a discipline nobody had fully appreciated until it showed up, all at once, as a single wire transfer with her name on it.

Eight months later, most of it is gone. Not recklessly, not in one visible catastrophe she could point to and explain — in dozens of small decisions that each felt, individually, defensible. New living room furniture, because the old set suddenly seemed unbearably shabby to sit in while grieving. A trip she and her sister took "for Mom," to a place their mother always wanted to see and never did, booked in first class because economy felt wrong for a trip taken in her memory. A kitchen renovation that started as replacing a cracked countertop and became, over six weeks of decisions made in a kind of fog, a full remodel, financed substantially by money that six months earlier had represented the last physical trace of her mother's entire working life. Somewhere in the middle of that stretch, she also started saying yes to things she'd normally have declined — a friend's destination birthday trip, a slightly-too-expensive dress for an event she didn't need to dress up for, a habit of picking up the tab at dinners that had, before the inheritance, always been split evenly. None of it felt like spending "the inheritance" in the moment. It felt like her regular life, mysteriously a little more expansive than it used to be. She does not regret any single purchase, exactly. She also cannot tell you, with any precision, where forty years of careful saving actually went, only that it went, and that some part of her suspects she let it go on purpose, because holding onto it too carefully felt like something she couldn't bear to do while still raw with the loss that produced it.

A different version of the same story, this one carrying an entirely different emotional charge: a man in his early fifties inherits a considerably larger sum from a father he had a difficult, distant relationship with — enough money that it could genuinely change the trajectory of his retirement, pay down his mortgage entirely, fund the early exit from a job he's disliked for a decade. The relationship with his father had been strained for most of his adult life, full of long silences and short, tense holiday visits, and the inheritance arrives less as an act of love than as a kind of posthumous obligation his father apparently felt but never expressed while he was alive to express it. The son doesn't grieve in any conventional sense — there's no acute wave of loss the way there was for the daughter in the kitchen — but there's something else instead, a complicated tangle of guilt, resentment, and unfinished business that the money seems to concentrate rather than resolve. Instead of quietly stewarding the inheritance, within two years most of it has gone into a business venture he'd never seriously considered before the money arrived — a restaurant, a passion project his father would have scoffed at, financed almost entirely by money he keeps calling, in conversation, "Dad's money," as though it retained his father's name on it even now, sitting in his own account. He talks about the restaurant, more than once, in language that sounds less like a business plan and more like a statement: proof, maybe, that he could build something his father never believed he had in him. The venture fails within eighteen months, undone by the ordinary difficulties every restaurant faces plus a set of decisions made with far less rigor than the man would ever have applied to his own earned savings. When it does fail, he describes the loss in a specific, telling way: not as losing his own retirement security, but as having "lost Dad's money" — language that reveals, more clearly than any survey could, that he never fully metabolized the inheritance as his own money at all. It arrived tagged with his father's identity, and he spent it, in some sense, as a referendum on that relationship rather than as a financial decision about his own future.

A third, quieter version of the pattern shows up in a sibling pair who inherit a family home, split evenly, following the death of both parents within a year of each other. Neither sibling needs the money urgently — both are financially stable, neither carries significant debt — and the sale of the house produces a moderate sum for each of them, nothing dramatic, nothing that changes either of their lives in any structural way. And yet both siblings, independently, without discussing it with each other beforehand, spend their respective shares within the same six-month window on almost identical categories: home improvements neither had budgeted for before the inheritance arrived, a family trip taken separately with their own households, a scattering of smaller purchases neither can fully account for a year later. When they eventually do compare notes, half-joking, about where the money went, neither can point to a single decision that felt like "spending Mom and Dad's house." Both describe something closer to a persistent, low-grade sense throughout that six-month stretch that money simply wasn't as tight as it usually was — a diffuse looseness rather than a series of deliberate choices, the inheritance dissolving not through any dramatic single decision but through months of ordinary life lived with slightly less resistance than usual.

A fourth version shows up at the opposite end of the life stage spectrum from the fifty-something son and the grieving daughter: a woman in her early twenties inherits a modest sum from a grandfather she was close to, the first significant money she's ever held that didn't come from a part-time job or a small graduation gift. She's a full year out of college, still finding her financial footing, sharing an apartment with two roommates and carrying a manageable amount of student debt she'd been chipping away at with something close to genuine discipline. The inheritance, while not large in absolute terms, is larger than anything she's ever had in a bank account at once, and it arrives at a life stage where she has almost no prior experience calibrating what a "large" sum should feel like or how carefully it deserves to be guarded. Where the older son's inheritance got tangled in a complicated relationship and the daughter's got tangled in acute grief, this young woman's version tangles with something different: a kind of financial vertigo, an inability to locate the money against any prior reference point in her own life, since she's never held anything remotely close to this amount before. She loved her grandfather uncomplicatedly, without the resentment or the acute fresh grief the other two cases carry, which means neither of the usual inheritance impulses — spend to honor, spend to be rid of the grief — applies cleanly to her situation. What applies instead is simpler and, in its own way, more universal: the money is so far outside her normal financial scale that she has no existing mental framework for treating it with the same care she'd apply to money she'd actually saved herself, dollar by modest dollar, from her entry-level salary. Within five months, roughly half of it funds a series of decisions she describes, without much self-judgment, as "finally getting to have nice things" — a better mattress, a solo trip she'd always wanted to take, a laptop upgrade she didn't strictly need but had been eyeing for over a year. None of these purchases are unreasonable on their own terms for someone starting to build an adult life. What's notable is that she never once compared any of them against what she'd have approved from her own paycheck, because the inheritance never got measured against that scale at all — it existed, from the moment it arrived, in a category so unfamiliar that her only real reference point for it was the unstructured freedom of finally having "enough," rather than any specific plan for what enough should actually accomplish for someone at her exact stage of life.

What's actually happening

Inheritance money carries a psychological complication that most other windfalls don't: it arrives braided together with loss, and grief itself changes decision-making in ways separate from, but compounding, the house money effect. The psychologist Richard Lazarus, whose work on stress and coping shaped how the field understands emotional response to major life disruption, described how intense grief narrows cognitive bandwidth and shifts a person toward what he termed emotion-focused coping — strategies aimed at managing the feeling of the loss itself rather than solving the practical problems the loss created. Spending, in this frame, isn't primarily a financial act at all during acute grief. It's frequently an emotional one, reached for because it offers something concrete and controllable in a period defined by how little control a person actually has over what's happened.

Layer the house money effect on top of that, and you get a specific, potent combination. The inherited money already carries none of the psychic cost of effortful earning — by the definition this whole book runs on, it's automatically coded as less real, easier to part with, than money built through the inheritor's own sustained work. But grief adds something the ordinary house money effect doesn't have on its own: a felt sense that the money is somehow still connected to the person who's gone, which produces two contradictory and equally costly impulses. One impulse treats the money as sacred, something that must be spent in a way that "honors" the deceased, which sounds noble and frequently justifies purchases — trips, renovations, gestures — far larger and less considered than the same person would ever make with their own earned income. The other impulse treats the money as almost radioactive, something to be rid of quickly because holding it too carefully feels, obscurely, disrespectful to the grief itself, as though careful budgeting would somehow diminish the loss. Both impulses point the same direction: toward spending the inheritance faster and less deliberately than an equivalent windfall arriving without grief attached.

Look closer at the son who kept calling his inheritance "Dad's money," and something else comes into focus. He was demonstrating something psychologists studying inheritance and bequests have observed directly: money inherited from a specific person, especially in a complicated relationship, often retains what researchers call a source tag — a persistent mental association with the giver that never fully dissolves the way the origin of an ordinary paycheck dissolves within weeks of receiving it. You know, roughly, where your salary came from, but it doesn't feel like it's still connected to your employer a year later. Inherited money can carry its source tag indefinitely, and when the relationship with that source was unresolved, complicated, or painful, spending the money — especially spending it in ways the source would have disapproved of — can function, unconsciously, as a delayed conversation with someone who's no longer available to have it. The restaurant wasn't really a business decision. It was, in part, an argument with a father who could no longer respond.

It's worth noticing that these two cases — the daughter's warm, straightforward grief and the son's tangled, unresolved resentment — produce the identical spending pattern despite pointing in almost opposite emotional directions. This is one of the more unsettling features of how inheritance money gets handled: it doesn't seem to matter much whether the underlying relationship was loving or difficult, resolved or estranged. What matters is that the money is entangled with a person who's no longer present to see how it's used, and that entanglement — regardless of its emotional flavor — appears to loosen the recipient's ordinary financial caution in strikingly similar ways. Grief spends it trying to hold on. Resentment spends it trying to prove something. Both spend it fast.

The young woman's case points to a distinct variant of the mechanism worth naming on its own terms, since it involves neither acute grief nor a complicated relationship: what researchers studying financial socialization call scale unfamiliarity, the simple absence of any prior lived experience against which to calibrate a sum of a given size. Most financial discipline is built incrementally, through repeated exposure to sums within a person's normal range — a twenty-something who has only ever budgeted paychecks in the hundreds or low thousands has no practiced internal calibration for what careful stewardship of a much larger sum actually looks like, in the same way a person's sense of "expensive" for a meal or a piece of clothing is anchored entirely by what they're used to encountering, not by any objective standard. A first-time large sum, inherited or otherwise, arrives outside that calibration entirely, and in the absence of any practiced internal scale for it, the mind reaches for the nearest available frame, which is very often simply "more than I've ever had," a description that carries no information at all about what careful use of that sum would actually require. This is part of why age and prior financial experience matter so much in how an inheritance gets handled: it isn't only about grief or relationship complexity, though both matter enormously where they're present. It's also, more simply, about whether the recipient has ever had to develop judgment at this particular scale before, and a first encounter with a new financial scale, whatever its emotional context, tends to get treated with less rigor than a scale a person has had years to grow into.

There's a final piece of the mechanism worth naming, connected to a broader finding in decision science about how people handle decisions made under acute emotional load more generally. Research on affective forecasting — the study of how accurately people predict their own future emotional states —

has repeatedly found that people are poor judges, in the moment of acute grief, of what will actually bring lasting relief versus what will bring only momentary distraction. The daughter's kitchen renovation and the son's restaurant were both, in their own ways, bets on a specific emotional forecast: that this purchase, this project, this gesture would meaningfully ease the weight they were carrying. Neither purchase delivered on that forecast in any durable way, which is the typical finding in this area of research — large purchases made to resolve emotional states tend to produce a brief lift followed by a return to baseline, while the emotional work the purchase was meant to substitute for remains, essentially, undone. Grief doesn't respond well to being outspent, no matter how sincerely the spending is intended.

What it costs you

The financial cost of inherited money spent this quickly is often larger than any other windfall category in this book, simply because inheritances tend to be larger sums than bonuses or refunds, arriving all at once rather than spread across a year. Money that could have meaningfully altered a person's financial trajectory — funding a genuine emergency reserve, paying down expensive debt, providing a foundation for the next decade — instead gets absorbed into a period of grief-driven spending that leaves little durable trace, and often leaves the inheritor in a worse position eighteen months later than they were the day the money arrived, because the psychological high of the windfall has worn off entirely while the financial reality it could have solved remains unsolved.

The quieter cost is what doesn't get built. An inheritance spent quickly in grief isn't just money lost — it's frequently the last physical connection to a life's worth of someone else's careful effort, dissolved without ever being consciously decided upon, dissolved by a fog rather than a choice. Many people who spend an inheritance this way report, months or years later, a specific kind of regret that's different from ordinary financial regret: not "I wish I'd invested that better," but something closer to "I wish I'd been more present when I decided what to do with it" — because they can sense, looking back, that they weren't really the one making the decisions during that period. Grief was.

There's also a cost specific to the complicated-relationship version of this pattern, one the son's story illustrates clearly. When inherited money gets spent as an unconscious argument with the person who left it, the spending rarely resolves the underlying feeling it was trying to address. The restaurant's failure didn't settle anything between the son and his father — if anything, it deepened the story he already carried about not being taken seriously, adding a fresh, concrete failure to a lifetime's worth of older, vaguer ones. Money spent trying to answer an emotional question it was never actually equipped to answer tends to leave both the money and the question gone, with nothing resolved on either side.

How this shows up without you noticing

The daughter's kitchen renovation didn't begin as a renovation. It began as a single cracked countertop, a genuinely reasonable, modest repair that any homeowner might have made regardless of any inheritance at all. The scope crept outward one decision at a time — since the counter's being redone, might as well handle the cabinets, since the cabinets are coming out, might as well address the floor — each individual expansion small enough to feel like simple thoroughness rather than a pattern worth questioning. This is usually how inheritance spending actually unfolds in real time: not as a single, nameable decision to "spend the inheritance," but as a sequence of individually modest expansions, each one justified on its own terms, that only add up to something large when looked at from a distance months later. If you notice a project, a trip, or a purchase quietly growing in scope after an inheritance arrives, that's usually the moment worth pausing at — not because growth is inherently wrong, but because it's rarely evaluated as growth while it's happening.

The overrides

Separate the timeline of grieving from the timeline of deciding. There is no financial emergency that requires an inheritance decision to be made in the first weeks or months after a loss, and treating the money as though there is one is almost always the grief talking, not the finances. Give yourself an explicit, extended waiting period — long enough to genuinely surface from the earliest, foggiest stage of loss — before making any large, discretionary decision with inherited money. This isn't about denying yourself. It's about making sure the person making the decision is you, clear-headed, rather than you, three weeks into acute grief.

Separate honoring the person from spending the money. If the impulse to "do something meaningful" with the inheritance arrives, examine it directly: does honoring this person actually require spending money, or is spending money simply the most available way to feel like you're doing something with an emotion that has nowhere else to go? Often, the most genuine tribute is stewarding what someone spent a lifetime building rather than dissolving it quickly — but only you can judge that honestly, and it's worth actually asking the question rather than assuming the answer.

Name the source tag if it's there, and decide consciously whether to keep it. If you notice yourself still calling the money by the giver's name months after receiving it — "Dad's money," "Grandma's money" — that's worth pausing on. It's not wrong to feel that connection. But recognize that as long as the money carries someone else's name in your mind, you may end up making decisions about it that are really about your relationship with them, rather than decisions about your own financial life. Sometimes the healthiest move is a small, symbolic act — moving the money into an account with your own name on the goal, treating one meaningful portion as an explicit tribute and the rest as simply yours — that lets you keep the memory without letting the memory keep making your financial decisions for you.

Bring in someone outside the grief to sanity-check large decisions. A trusted friend, a sibling who isn't as deep in the fog, or a financial professional with no emotional stake in the estate can often see the gap between what you're deciding and what you'd decide with a clear head far more easily than you can see it yourself in the middle of loss. This isn't about ceding the decision to someone else — it's about giving the clear-headed version of yourself, the one who'll exist again in six months, a voice in a decision being made before she's fully back.

Watch for scope creep in any single project funded by the inheritance. If a modest, reasonable repair or purchase starts quietly expanding — a countertop becomes a full remodel, a small tribute becomes a first-class trip — pause and ask whether the expansion reflects a genuine, considered decision or simply the absence of the resistance that would normally slow such expansions down. Scope creep during grief is common precisely because there's no natural stopping point once the first expansion has already been rationalized.

If this is the largest sum of money you've ever held, borrow a scale from somewhere else before inventing your own. When an inheritance outpaces anything you've had prior experience managing, don't rely on your gut sense of what careful stewardship looks like at this new size — it likely doesn't exist yet. Ask what a financially disciplined person several years further into their career would do with the identical sum, or talk through the number, plainly, with someone whose judgment you trust and who has actually managed money at this scale before. Borrowing a calibration is far safer than inventing one under the emotional weight of a fresh loss.

If you're currently settling an estate, write down what the money represents before deciding what to do with it. Not the dollar figure — the actual life it came from. A sentence or two about what this person built, sacrificed, or valued in order to leave this behind. Keep that sentence somewhere you'll see it during the months ahead. It won't stop grief from wanting to spend quickly, but it gives the money a story that's harder to dissolve carelessly than an anonymous number in an account ever could be.

Rule to remember: *grief will try to make financial decisions on your behalf if you let it hold the checkbook too soon. Let yourself grieve fully before you let yourself decide — the money will still be there, and so, in every way that matters, will they.*

Chapter 3 — The Bonus

Why Reward Money Feels Like Permission Instead of Pay

The email arrives at 4:47 on a Friday afternoon in December, subject line something bland and corporate — "Year-End Compensation Update" — and by the time he's finished reading it, something in his posture has changed. Twelve thousand dollars, on top of his regular salary, landing in two weeks. He closes the laptop and sits very still for a moment, the way you sit still right after hearing genuinely good news, letting it settle before you let yourself react to it. Then he opens a browser tab and starts looking at a watch he's wanted for three years — nothing extravagant by the standards of watches, but well beyond anything he'd normally let himself consider, filed for years under "someday, maybe, if things ever loosen up."

He tells his wife over dinner, and her first reaction, practical as always, is relief — the roof needs attention before winter, and this solves that without touching their regular savings plan. He agrees, in the moment, and means it. But over the following days, a second conversation starts running quietly alongside the practical one, a conversation he doesn't fully share with her: a sense that he's earned, specifically, the right to enjoy some of this himself, separately from what it does for the household. He worked harder this year than he can remember working in a long time — the late nights, the strained months on a difficult project, the year his manager specifically cited in the bonus letter as the reason for the number. Surely some portion of that recognition is his, personally, to spend on something that has nothing to do with the roof.

Here's the specific shape of what happens next, and it's worth being precise about it, because the mechanism hides in the precision. He doesn't think of the twelve thousand dollars as pay for work he already did — which is, factually, exactly what it is, a formal recognition of a year's performance, negotiated and calculated the same way his salary was. He thinks of it as a reward, a gift from the company, something extra that exists outside the normal category of "money I earn to live on." And reward money, once it's been mentally filed that way, comes pre-loaded with an unspoken permission: reward money is for treating yourself. Salary is for obligations. The distinction exists nowhere in the actual accounting — his employer withheld the same taxes, wired it to the same account, and it spends identically to every other dollar he's ever earned. The distinction exists entirely in his head, and it's about to cost him considerably more than the price of a watch. By the time the roof is paid for, the watch has been purchased, along with a handful of smaller "since I'm at it" additions — a strap, a second, less expensive watch he decides he also deserves, dinner out to celebrate the whole thing — and the twelve thousand dollars, which had a specific, practical, agreed-upon purpose the night it arrived, has been stretched considerably further than either he or his wife discussed.

A different version of the pattern, this one without a partner in the room to provide even the brief moment of practical framing the roof conversation offered: a woman running a small landscaping business has her best year yet, and rather than a formal year-end bonus, she pays herself a substantial owner's distribution once the books are finalized — money that is, in every meaningful sense, exactly as earned as any invoice she billed all year, arguably more directly earned, since it represents the actual profit of a business she built herself, absorbing risk no salaried employee absorbs. And yet she describes it, to her sister, using language strikingly similar to the man with the watch: "I finally get to have some fun with it." Not "this is what the business generated this year, on top of what I already paid myself" — "fun money," as though the distribution existed in a category separate from the labor that produced it. Over the following two months, a chunk of that distribution goes toward a truck upgrade she'd been debating for a year, a set of home renovations that had been "someday" projects, and a family trip that, by her own later accounting, cost nearly double what she'd have approved if she'd been drawing from the business's regular operating cushion instead of from what she'd mentally filed as a bonus. When her accountant, reviewing the year-end numbers the following spring, gently points out that the distribution was substantially larger than what she'd set aside for the following year's tax liability, she's genuinely surprised — not because she didn't know the distribution was large, but because she'd never quite connected the size of the "fun money" to the size of the obligation it was supposed to help cover. Same business. Same owner. Same money, dollar for dollar. Different category in her head, and a completely different level of scrutiny applied to spending it.

A third case shows the same mechanism at a smaller, more frequent scale: a restaurant server who receives cash tips nightly treats that income as functionally different from her hourly wage, even though both fund the identical rent and groceries at the end of the month. The hourly wage, paid biweekly by direct deposit, gets budgeted carefully — she knows almost to the dollar what it needs to cover. The tips, handed to her in cash across dozens of small transactions throughout each shift, get spent far more loosely, absorbed into daily incidentals, impulse purchases on the way home, rounds of drinks with coworkers after a long night, in a pattern she's never once sat down and actually totaled. When a slow month at the restaurant leaves her short on rent, she's caught off guard, because in her own mental accounting the tips were never quite counted as "real income" that needed protecting — they were treated, consistently, as a nightly bonus for a hard shift, spent according to bonus rules rather than paycheck rules, despite regularly making up nearly half her actual monthly earnings.

A fourth case shows how the pattern scales up rather than down: a sales director who earns a large chunk of her annual compensation through quarterly commission, paid out as a lump sum each quarter based on the previous three months' closed deals. Unlike a once-a-year bonus, this happens four times annually, which one might expect would eventually train it into feeling like ordinary income through sheer repetition. It doesn't. Each quarterly payout arrives with the identical fresh burst of "extra money" feeling the first one ever did, regardless of how many times she's now lived through the cycle, and each one gets spent with a similar looseness — a nicer vacation this quarter, a home upgrade the next, rarely the same disciplined treatment she applies to her modest base salary, which she budgets with genuine precision. The repetition of the windfall, rather than habituating her discipline the way repeated exposure to most experiences eventually does, seems to simply repeat the same lapse in discipline four times a year instead of once.

A fifth case shows the pattern operating in a context that has nothing to do with rewarding past performance at all: a software engineer in his early thirties accepts a new position that includes a signing bonus roughly equal to three months of take-home pay, structured explicitly by the new employer as an incentive to accept the offer rather than as compensation for any work performed yet. The money arrives in his first paycheck, before he's completed a single full month in the role, which gives it a psychological quality none of the other bonuses in this chapter quite share: it isn't even retroactively earned in the loose sense a year-end bonus is. It's forward-facing, a bet the company is making on him, and he describes it, tellingly, as "basically free money to start things off right." He and his partner had discussed, before the offer was even signed, putting the signing bonus toward closing costs on a home they'd been saving toward for two years — a specific, agreed-upon plan formed before the money's arrival could cloud the decision. But once the deposit actually posts, sitting in an account that, three days later, is nearly four times its usual balance, the plan starts to feel less binding than it did in the abstract. He finds himself, within the first month at the new job, upgrading his home office setup considerably beyond what the role requires, buying a bicycle he'd mentioned wanting "eventually," and treating a run of restaurant dinners with new colleagues as a natural, low-stakes way to build relationships in his first weeks — each individually reasonable, collectively eating into the exact fund the money had been earmarked for before it ever arrived. When he and his partner finally sit down to move money toward the closing costs two months later, the signing bonus has shrunk by nearly a third, and he's genuinely surprised, since none of the individual purchases had felt, in the moment, like touching "the house money" at all — they'd felt like the ordinary texture of starting a new chapter, funded, invisibly, by a sum that had never actually been treated as spoken-for despite having been explicitly discussed as such before it even arrived.

What's actually happening

The mental shift both of these people made — from "earned pay" to "reward" — has a specific behavioral-economics explanation, and it connects directly back to the mental accounting framework Richard Thaler mapped across decades of research. Thaler's work established that people don't just sort money by amount; they sort it by the emotional category attached to how it arrived, and different categories get assigned different implicit spending rules regardless of the money's actual fungibility. A bonus gets filed, almost automatically, into a category adjacent to "windfall" rather than "income," even though structurally it is income, calculated and taxed exactly like the rest of a salary. The word itself does some of the damage — "bonus" linguistically implies something extra, above and beyond, outside the baseline, and that framing primes the brain to treat the money as available for above-and-beyond spending before a single dollar has actually been evaluated on its own merits.

This connects to a related finding from research on hedonic framing — how the way a gain is presented changes the pleasure derived from spending it, and how much scrutiny people apply before spending it. Money framed as a reward for effort already expended carries an implicit message: you've already done the hard part, this is the payoff, and payoffs are supposed to be enjoyed rather than deliberated over. Compare that to how the same person would treat an unexpected instruction from their employer to simply defer twelve thousand dollars of regular salary — an identical sum, differently framed — and you'd likely see far more caution, far more of the ordinary planning process a person applies to their regular paycheck. The bonus escapes that scrutiny specifically because of its framing as a reward rather than as deferred, ordinary pay, and companies, whether or not they intend to, reinforce this framing constantly, describing bonuses in language of gifts, recognition, and celebration rather than in the plain language of compensation.

There's a compounding effect here too, one that connects back to the reference-point mechanism from Chapter 1. A bonus typically arrives as a single, visible lump sum rather than smoothed across pay periods the way salary is — and a lump sum, psychologically, reads as a windfall event even when its underlying source is ordinary, earned income. The size and suddenness of the deposit trigger the same house money coding that an inheritance or a lottery win would trigger, layered directly on top of money that, unlike an actual windfall, really did require the sustained effort this whole book distinguishes windfalls from. The bonus is, in a sense, the hardest case in this book precisely because it sits on the boundary — genuinely earned, but psychologically windfall-coded by its delivery format, and the psychology wins the argument almost every time.

The man's roof conversation reveals one more piece of the mechanism. Look at the way a bonus gets mentally split, almost immediately, into a "responsible" portion and a "mine" portion, even when no such split exists in the actual compensation letter. His employer didn't earmark part of the twelve thousand dollars for the roof and part of it for personal enjoyment — that division happened entirely inside his own head, in the seconds after the practical conversation with his wife concluded. This self-imposed split matters because it creates a psychological permission structure: once the "responsible" portion has been assigned, the recipient often feels they've fully discharged their financial duty, freeing the remainder for spending with even less scrutiny than an ordinary discretionary purchase would receive, because it's already been mentally certified as the "fun" share, earned twice over — once through the work, and again through having behaved responsibly with the rest.

The server's tip pattern points to a related idea, one with its own name in the research: moral licensing, studied across behavioral economics and social psychology, which describes how a virtuous act in one domain can create a subjective sense of permission to act less carefully in another, even when the two domains have no logical connection. Behaving responsibly with the hourly wage — budgeting it carefully, treating it with the seriousness a bill-paying paycheck deserves — appears to generate exactly this kind of license for the tips, as though the discipline applied to one income stream banks a kind of credit that can be spent, guilt-free, on looseness with the other. The two income streams are, of course, entirely fungible in reality; nothing about being careful with one actually earns any slack with the other. But moral licensing doesn't run on actual fungibility. It runs on a felt sense of having already been good enough for the day, and that felt sense is precisely what a bonus's "responsible portion, fun portion" split manufactures on a larger scale.

The signing-bonus example is precise about why this happens: it shows that even an explicit, mutually agreed-upon plan formed before a windfall arrives isn't automatically immune to the pattern this chapter describes. Behavioral researchers studying commitment devices — pre-decided plans intended to bind future behavior — have found that such plans are considerably more effective when they're structurally enforced, meaning the money is physically or procedurally moved out of easy reach, than when they rely purely on memory and willpower once the money is sitting, liquid and visible, in an everyday account. The engineer and his partner had a plan, and the plan was genuine. What they didn't have was any structural mechanism forcing the money to actually go where the plan said, which meant the plan was competing, day after day, against a fully liquid balance and a fresh, exciting life chapter — a competition a purely mental commitment usually loses by inches, one reasonable-seeming purchase at a time, rather than through any single decision to abandon the plan outright. This is a useful corrective to the assumption that simply deciding what to do with a bonus in advance is sufficient protection; deciding is necessary, but deciding without also removing the money from convenient reach leaves the decision to compete, unaided, against every one of the small temptations bonus money reliably produces.

What it costs you

The direct cost is straightforward and repeats every single review cycle for people who fall into this pattern: a meaningful chunk of annual compensation, treated as consumption money rather than as what it structurally is — a large, lump-sum addition to annual income that could be allocated with the same seriousness applied to the rest of a salary — gets spent on purchases that wouldn't have survived the scrutiny applied to regular paycheck spending. Multiply that gap across a decade of bonus cycles and the difference between treating bonus money as pay versus treating it as reward becomes one of the largest single levers in most people's entire financial trajectory, larger in raw dollar terms than most of the smaller daily spending decisions that get far more attention in conventional financial advice.

The subtler cost is what the reward-framing does to a person's relationship with their own hard work. If the bonus is mentally coded as separate from "real" income — as a gift rather than as compensation you actually earned through a year of sustained effort — then spending it recklessly starts to feel disconnected from the effort that produced it, which quietly erodes the sense that hard work translates into durable results. The landscaping business owner worked exactly as hard to generate her distribution as she worked to generate every invoice throughout the year. Treating the distribution as a separate, lesser-scrutinized category doesn't just cost her money — it subtly undercuts the very story she should be telling herself about what her effort actually built.

A third cost shows up specifically in households where bonuses are a recurring, expected part of annual compensation. Over time, a pattern of treating bonus season as separate from ordinary financial planning can create a structural gap in a household's actual security: the regular budget gets built around salary alone, as though the bonus doesn't reliably exist, while the bonus itself gets spent as though it were never meant to be planned around in the first place. This leaves many households in the strange position of having a considerably larger total annual income than their actual financial resilience would suggest, because a meaningful fraction of that income never gets folded into the infrastructure — the emergency fund, the retirement contributions, the debt payoff plan — that the rest of the income is quietly building. The bonus arrives every year, and every year it behaves like a surprise, which means the household never gets to benefit from planning around a predictable, recurring resource the way it could if the bonus were simply treated as part of the annual total from the outset.

How this shows up without you noticing

The clearest tell is the language itself, and it's worth listening for it in your own head as much as anyone else's. Any time you catch yourself thinking or saying "I finally get to have some fun with it" about money that is, structurally, ordinary compensation, that phrase is doing exactly the work this chapter has been describing — building a wall between "money I earned" and "money I'm allowed to enjoy without scrutiny" that doesn't correspond to anything real about the money itself. The watch, the truck upgrade, the "since I'm at it" additions — none of these announce themselves as bonus spending while they're happening. They announce themselves as reasonable, proportionate treats, each one small enough on its own to escape the kind of scrutiny you'd apply if the identical purchase were being weighed against four weeks of regular paycheck money instead.

A second, quieter tell shows up in how quickly the conversation about a bonus shifts from planning to spending. Notice the gap, or lack of one, between "the bonus is coming" and "here's what I'm going to buy with it." A genuinely deliberate process usually has some visible friction in it — a comparison, a delay, a second opinion sought. If a bonus routes straight from anticipation to a specific purchase with no visible deliberation in between, that speed itself is diagnostic, since ordinary paycheck-funded purchases of similar size rarely move that fast.

The overrides

Rename it in your own language before you let yourself plan anything with it. The moment a bonus, distribution, or lump-sum reward arrives, consciously relabel it, out loud or in writing: this is pay for work I already did, not a gift on top of my real income. Companies will keep calling it a bonus. You don't have to adopt their framing as your own internal accounting.

Apply your ordinary paycheck rules to it, deliberately, before applying any exceptions. Whatever process you'd normally run a regular paycheck through — savings allocation, debt paydown, planned versus discretionary spending — run the bonus through the identical process first, before carving out any "treat yourself" portion. If a genuine celebration portion still makes sense after that, decide on it consciously and specifically, rather than letting the entire sum default into the reward category by not deciding at all.

Split it the moment it lands, before the reward feeling has time to take hold. The house money effect has less room to operate on money that's already been moved somewhere less liquid and less visible in your day-to-day spending. Moving a portion — decided in advance, before the deposit even posts — into something less immediately accessible removes the ongoing daily temptation of watching a large, "extra" balance sit in a checking account, quietly inviting a reward mindset every time you check it.

Watch for the self-granted split that lets the rest off the hook. If you notice yourself mentally dividing a bonus into a "responsible" chunk and a "mine" chunk, examine the mine chunk with exactly the same scrutiny you gave the responsible one, rather than treating the act of being responsible with part of it as a license to stop thinking carefully about the rest. Responsibility with one portion isn't a coupon that buys carelessness with another.

If your income includes irregular components like tips or commission, fold them into your real budget rather than treating them as bonus-adjacent. Any income that arrives outside the predictable, itemized structure of a base wage is especially vulnerable to this chapter's pattern, precisely because its irregularity makes it easy to treat as supplemental rather than essential. Track it, average it, and budget against the average, the same way you would if it arrived as a single predictable number each pay period.

Make your plan structural, not just mental, whenever the bonus is earmarked for something specific. A plan that lives only in a conversation or a shared understanding is fighting the house money effect with no real defenses. The moment a bonus posts, move the earmarked portion immediately into a separate account, a dedicated savings vehicle, or anything that adds a genuine step between the money and your everyday spending — the friction itself is doing real protective work that willpower alone reliably fails to do once the balance is sitting there, liquid and visible, every time you check it.

If a bonus is coming, write your allocation plan down before the deposit posts, and share it with someone. A plan that exists only in your head, formed in the excitement of anticipation, is far easier to quietly revise downward — a little here, a little there — than a plan that's been written down and, ideally, said out loud to a partner or a friend who can gently ask, weeks later, whether the plan actually held.

Rule to remember: *a bonus is not a gift from your employer — it's the part of your salary that arrived all at once instead of spread across the year. Treat it with the same seriousness you'd treat any other paycheck, and let the celebration be a conscious decision, not a default.*

Chapter 4 — The Refund

Why Your Own Money Feels Like Someone Else's Gift

The notification arrives in early March: your federal refund has been deposited. Two thousand four hundred dollars, give or take, landing in an account that, three days earlier, held considerably less. There's a specific lightness to seeing that number appear — a feeling genuinely indistinguishable, in the moment, from the feeling of winning something. It is not winning anything. It is the government returning money that was always yours, withheld from your own paychecks across the previous year because your employer, by law, took out more than you actually owed. Every dollar of that refund was earned, by you, in the ordinary way, over fifty-two ordinary weeks. It simply took a detour through the government's hands before completing its trip back to you.

None of that changes how it feels landing in the account. Within an hour of the deposit notification, a woman in her late twenties has three browser tabs open — flights for a trip she'd mentioned wanting to take "eventually," a pair of boots she'd been eyeing since November, and a gift for her partner's upcoming birthday, upgraded from what she'd been planning to something considerably nicer, "since there's a little extra this year." She scrolls back through her banking app, briefly, to look at what her actual paycheck deposits looked like across the previous year — steady, familiar, carefully tracked in the spreadsheet she updates every Sunday night — and then looks back at the refund notification, sitting there looking almost identical in format, and feels nothing of the same caution toward it at all. Not one of these purchases would have survived contact with her regular budgeting process, the one she actually uses for her paycheck, where she tracks categories carefully and asks herself, genuinely, whether each discretionary purchase is worth deferring something else for. The refund skips that entire process. It arrives already coded, in her mind, as bonus money, found money, a small windfall the government handed her — rather than as the exact same paycheck dollars she was disciplined about eleven months earlier when they first left her employer's payroll system. By the end of the month, the flights are booked, the boots are on their way, and the birthday gift has been upgraded twice more since her first idea, each upgrade justified by the same phrase — there's a little extra this year — applied to a shrinking pool of money that was never actually extra to begin with.

A second version, further along the same pattern: a family expecting a considerably larger refund due to a child tax credit treats the anticipated deposit, months before it even arrives, as already spoken for in a way their regular income never gets treated. Around the dinner table in January, well before any filing has even been completed, they've discussed a larger television, a portion toward a used car upgrade, a family trip — conversations they would never have about an equivalent sum arriving as four extra weeks of ordinary paychecks, because four extra weeks of ordinary paychecks would immediately get absorbed into the household's actual, ongoing obligations rather than discussed as a discrete pool available for wants. The father, in particular, has taken to referring to the anticipated refund as "our bonus" in these conversations, a phrase his wife doesn't correct, though she works in bookkeeping and knows, professionally, exactly what a tax refund actually represents. When the refund arrives and turns out to be roughly what they expected, the spending proceeds close to plan — not because the plan was carefully evaluated, but because it had already been agreed to, months earlier, based purely on the anticipation of "extra" money that was never actually extra at all. Meanwhile, the emergency fund they've discussed building "someday" for three consecutive years remains exactly where it was in January, because it never once entered the conversation about what to do with the refund — an omission that would have been unthinkable if the same sum had arrived as a raise.

A third, smaller-scale version shows up in a college student who receives a modest refund from an overpayment on tuition, money that was, unambiguously, hers to begin with, sitting briefly with the university's financial office before being returned. The amount is small enough that it barely registers as a financial event at all, and yet it gets spent within days on a night out with friends, a purchase she wouldn't have made from her part-time job earnings without a longer internal negotiation first. She describes the refund, without any hesitation, as "extra money the school gave me back" — a phrasing that erases, entirely, the fact that the money was hers from the moment she first paid it, months earlier, out of her own account. The smallness of the sum doesn't diminish the pattern. If anything, it demonstrates how automatically the mechanism runs, requiring neither a large amount nor a complicated backstory to fully take hold.

A fourth version, closer to the scale of the family's child-tax-credit refund, shows up in a self-employed contractor who overestimates his quarterly tax payments across a slow year and receives a meaningful refund the following spring when he finally files. Because his income is irregular by nature, he's long since stopped mentally tracking each dollar back to a specific invoice or project, which makes the refund feel even more disconnected from any identifiable source than a typical employee's refund would. He describes it, to his accountant, as "a nice surprise," language that quietly reclassifies a full year of his own overpaid labor as a stroke of luck rather than as a correction to his own estimate. Within a month, a meaningful share of it funds equipment upgrades he'd been putting off — not unreasonable purchases in themselves, but ones he'd have subjected to considerably more comparison-shopping and deliberation had the money arrived as ordinary invoice income instead of as a single detached refund check.

A fifth version shows the pattern persisting even among people who have decades of financial experience behind them: a retired couple in their late sixties, both former accountants, have filed their own taxes carefully every year of their working lives and understand, in precise technical detail, exactly what a refund represents. Neither would describe themselves as naive about withholding mechanics. And yet, every spring, the arrival of their refund — typically modest, since they've adjusted their withholding fairly close to accurate over the years — still produces a distinct, separate "refund conversation" at their kitchen table, one that has its own tone and its own looser rules compared to how they discuss the rest of their fixed retirement income. This year's refund funds a slightly more elaborate version of their annual trip to visit grandchildren, complete with upgraded flights neither would have booked from their regular monthly budget without a longer conversation about whether it was worth it. When their daughter, visiting for the holidays, asks whether the flight upgrade came out of their regular travel budget, her mother laughs and says, "No, that was refund money" — a distinction her daughter finds curious, since she knows both her parents understand, better than almost anyone, exactly where a refund actually comes from. The couple's technical knowledge of the mechanism turns out to offer no particular immunity to the mechanism itself; understanding the flypaper effect intellectually and feeling its pull are, it turns out, two entirely separate things, and the second one operates largely independent of the first.

What's actually happening

The tax refund is, in a sense, the purest test case in this entire book for the house money effect, because it strips away every variable the other chapters have to work around. There's no grief complicating it, as with an inheritance. There's no genuine ambiguity about whether it was earned, as there sometimes is with a gift. It is, unambiguously, wages you already worked for, withheld and returned in full. And it still gets spent like a windfall, almost universally, which tells you the mechanism doesn't actually track whether money was earned — it tracks the felt experience of the money's arrival, and a refund arrives exactly like a windfall arrives: as a single, unscheduled, unearned-feeling lump sum, disconnected in time and format from the paycheck cycle that actually produced it.

Richard Thaler's mental accounting framework explains this precisely: money gets sorted not by its true origin but by the context of its arrival, and a refund arrives in a context — a government deposit, once a year, disconnected from any specific pay stub, often for an amount the recipient can't easily trace back to specific withheld paychecks — that mimics every surface feature of a windfall even though its underlying source is the least windfall-like source imaginable. The disconnection in time is doing real work here. If your employer withheld an extra fifty dollars from every paycheck and then handed it back to you, dollar for dollar, at the end of each pay period, you would never experience that fifty dollars as a windfall — you'd experience it as your paycheck being what it always should have been. Stretch that same withholding across a full year and deliver it in a single detached deposit, and the same dollars, tracing back to the same source, get an entirely different psychological treatment.

There's a specific research finding here, from the study of what economists call the flypaper effect in household spending — the observation that money "sticks" to whatever mental category it arrives labeled as, spent according to that category's implicit rules rather than pooled rationally with all other household income the way a purely rational actor would treat it. A tax refund is one of the most studied instances of this effect in the consumer spending literature, and the consistent finding is that refunds get spent at meaningfully higher rates on discretionary and non-essential purchases than equivalent amounts of regular income, even among households who describe themselves, accurately, as careful budgeters in every other part of their financial life. The refund isn't tested against the same mental bar. It gets a pass, purely because of its label and its delivery format, that the household's ordinary income never gets.

The family's dinner-table conversations reveal a further wrinkle: anticipation itself appears to lock in the windfall coding well before the money even arrives. By the time the refund actually landed, the "our bonus" framing had been rehearsed at that table for months, giving the house money effect a running head start it doesn't get with a bonus or a settlement, which typically arrive with less lead time for the recipient to pre-commit, conversationally, to a windfall-spending mindset. The earlier and more explicitly a family discusses an anticipated refund as separate, discretionary money, the harder it becomes, by the time the deposit actually posts, to treat it as anything else — the mental category was fully built and furnished long before the money that was supposed to fill it ever showed up.

There's a related anchoring effect worth naming, drawn from the same broader tradition of judgment research that produced prospect theory. Once a household has estimated, informally, what a refund will likely be — based on the prior year's number, or a rough sense from a tax preparer — that estimate becomes an anchor the eventual spending plan gets built around, regardless of whether the anchor was ever a particularly accurate prediction. The family in this chapter anchored on "about what we got last year, maybe a bit more with the credit," and their spending conversations proceeded from that anchor as though it were a confirmed fact months before the actual number existed. This is a small but telling example of how thoroughly a windfall's psychological treatment can be locked in before the windfall itself has even technically arrived — the anticipation alone is often sufficient to fully activate the pattern this chapter describes.

The contractor's example adds one final piece worth naming: irregular income earners face a version of this chapter's pattern that salaried employees rarely encounter, because their entire relationship to "overpayment" is built on estimation rather than fixed withholding. A salaried employee's withholding is calculated by a payroll system according to fairly standard tables; a self-employed person's quarterly estimate is a guess, revised imperfectly year to year, and a large refund often reflects nothing more than a conservative guess proven too conservative. Because that guess was the contractor's own, rather than an employer's, the resulting refund carries an odd double coding: it's simultaneously his own money, chosen and set aside by his own estimate, and yet it still arrives with all the surface features of an external windfall — a single, detached, unscheduled deposit disconnected from any specific invoice.

This double coding may partly explain why self-employed refund spending can be just as loose as salaried refund spending, despite the recipient having had, in principle, far more visibility into exactly where the money came from.

The retired couple's case points to something worth naming explicitly, since it cuts against an assumption many readers of this book might otherwise make: that simply knowing the mechanism intellectually is sufficient to defuse it. Psychologists distinguish between what's sometimes called declarative knowledge — the kind of explicit, statable understanding a person could recite on request — and the automatic, largely unconscious processing that actually governs moment-to-moment behavior, and a substantial body of research on dual-process reasoning has found that the two systems operate with a surprising degree of independence from each other. A person can hold accurate, detailed declarative knowledge of exactly how a refund is generated — as two former accountants certainly do — while their automatic processing continues to categorize the deposit using the same windfall-coding shortcut this whole book describes, because that shortcut was never actually installed through explicit reasoning in the first place, and explicit reasoning alone doesn't reliably uninstall it. This is a sobering finding for a book that is, itself, an attempt to change behavior through explanation: understanding the house money effect, thoroughly and accurately, is a necessary step, but it is not, on its own, a sufficient one. The overrides throughout this book exist precisely because knowing the mechanism and interrupting the mechanism are different tasks, requiring different kinds of effort — and the couple's annual "refund conversation" is a useful, humbling reminder that expertise in the subject matter offers less protection than it might seem to promise.

What it costs you

The direct cost compounds across a working lifetime in a way that's easy to underestimate, because any single year's refund often isn't a dramatic sum — a few hundred, a couple thousand dollars, nothing that feels, in isolation, like a major financial event. But treated as spendable windfall money year after year, across two or three decades of a working life, the aggregate difference between refund-as-windfall and refund-as-delayed-paycheck represents a genuinely significant sum, one that, allocated with the same seriousness as regular income across that span, could have meaningfully funded a real goal instead of dissolving, invisibly, one modest impulse purchase per spring.

There's a second, less obvious cost specific to refunds: the withholding itself. Choosing to have your employer withhold more than you actually owe, rather than adjusting your withholding to more closely match your real tax liability, means giving the government an interest-free loan of your own money for up to a year, in exchange for the specific psychological experience of an annual "windfall" you can then spend without the scrutiny you'd apply to your regular paycheck. Many people, on some level, understand this trade-off and continue making it anyway, not from ignorance but because the annual windfall feeling is, in its own way, valuable enough to them that they're implicitly paying for it with lost access to their own money for months at a time. That's a legitimate choice if made consciously. It's a much more costly one when made by default, without ever noticing that's the trade being made.

There's a third cost worth naming, specific to households that lean on the refund as an informal savings mechanism — a pattern more common than it might sound, where a family effectively uses over-withholding as a forced-savings plan precisely because they don't trust themselves to set the equivalent amount aside on their own throughout the year. This isn't irrational; for some households, it genuinely works better than the alternative, because the friction of accessing the money is higher when it's tied up with the government than when it's sitting in an easily raided savings account. But if the money that arrives through this mechanism then gets spent with windfall-level looseness the moment it lands, the entire point of the forced-savings strategy is undone in the final step — all the discipline of the withholding period gets erased in a few weeks of spending that never got the scrutiny the withholding period was implicitly counting on.

How this shows up without you noticing

Watch for the specific vocabulary that surrounds a refund in the weeks before it lands — "when the refund comes," "we'll figure that out with the refund," "let's wait for tax season" —

because that vocabulary reveals whether the money is already being treated as a separate, discretionary category before it has even arrived. The browser-tab moment in this chapter's opening scene is a useful diagnostic in its own right: if a deposit notification sends you straight to shopping tabs before it sends you to your regular budgeting process, that's the tell, regardless of how small or large the amount actually is. The absence of the pause is the pattern.

A second tell worth watching for is how a refund gets described after the fact, once it's already spent. If you find yourself unable to answer, with any real specificity, where a refund from even a few months ago actually went, that vagueness itself is diagnostic. Money that passed through your regular, deliberate budgeting process tends to leave a traceable story — you can usually say what it did. Money that skipped that process, coded as a windfall from the start, tends to leave only a blur, which is exactly the shape refund spending takes for most people, most years.

The overrides

Say the true sentence before you spend a dollar of it. Before any refund gets touched, say the accurate version of what it is, out loud if you have to: this is my own wages, withheld too aggressively and returned to me late, not extra money the government is giving me. It sounds almost pedantic to insist on this, but the entire vanishing act depends on the softer, inaccurate framing — insisting on the accurate one is most of the work.

Route it through your regular income process instead of treating it as a separate decision. Whatever process governs how you allocate your paycheck — savings first, obligations next, discretionary last — apply that same process to the refund before carving out anything special. If it would take four weeks of paycheck-level scrutiny to approve a purchase from regular income, give the refund-funded version of that same purchase the same scrutiny, rather than a pass simply because of where the money technically came from.

Consider whether the annual windfall feeling is actually worth the trade you're making for it. If you value the specific experience of an annual refund enough to justify over-withholding all year to get it, that's a legitimate preference — but make sure it's a preference you've actually examined, rather than a default you've never questioned. If it isn't worth the trade, adjusting your withholding so the money arrives in your regular paychecks, where it's far more likely to get the scrutiny your actual budgeting process applies, is a more reliable way to make sure the money survives contact with your life.

Interrupt the anticipation conversation before the money even arrives. If you find yourself discussing an expected refund as though it's already spoken for — a bigger television, a trip, an upgrade — notice that the windfall coding is already locking in, months before the deposit posts. Reframe those conversations the way you'd reframe a conversation about an anticipated raise: worth planning for seriously, not worth pre-spending casually.

If you're self-employed or irregularly paid, treat an overpayment refund as evidence to correct your estimate, not as a surprise to spend. A recurring pattern of significant refunds usually means your quarterly or estimated payments are consistently set too high — the correct response is adjusting the estimate going forward, not celebrating the annual return of your own overpaid money as if it were a stroke of luck.

Do the math on your own withholding pattern, once, honestly. Pull the last two or three years of refund amounts and add them up. Seeing the actual total — money that sat with the government, interest-free, before quietly funding a handful of forgotten purchases — tends to do more to change behavior than any abstract description of the pattern, because it replaces a vague sense of "I get a nice refund most years" with a specific number that's harder to wave away.

Rule to remember: *a refund isn't a gift — it's your own paycheck arriving late, in a costume that makes it look like a windfall. Recognize the costume, and spend the money like the wages it always was.*

Chapter 5 — The Settlement

Why Money Attached to an Injury Gets Spent Like It's Trying to Disappear

He gets the call from his attorney on a Tuesday afternoon: the case has settled, and in three to five weeks, a figure he'd started to think might never actually materialize will land in his account — compensation for a car accident eighteen months earlier that left him with a shoulder that still aches in cold weather and a fear of highway on-ramps he's never fully shaken. The number is significant, larger than anything he's held at once in his life. His first feeling, when the check finally clears, isn't relief. It's something closer to nausea — a strange, unwanted intimacy with the exact dollar value his own pain apparently carries, a number that makes the whole ordeal feel simultaneously validated and cheapened, like the eighteen months of physical therapy and missed work and highway anxiety have been reduced to a figure that both means everything and somehow doesn't feel like enough.

For the first two weeks, the money simply sits, untouched, while he goes about a version of his normal routine that feels strange now, punctuated by moments where he catches himself staring at the account balance without quite deciding to. His wife raises the subject carefully, at dinner one night, wondering aloud whether they should talk to someone about how to use it — a financial planner, maybe, given the size of the sum and the fact that neither of them has ever managed anything close to this much money at once. He agrees in principle and does nothing about it, and the conversation doesn't come up again for weeks, crowded out by an accumulating series of smaller decisions that don't feel, individually, like they're using "the settlement money" at all.

Within four months, the majority of it is gone. A truck, considerably nicer than the one that was totaled in the accident, paid for close to outright — a purchase he frames, to himself and to his wife, as simply replacing what the accident took, even though the new truck is a full trim level above the one that was destroyed. A series of purchases for his kids that he describes, when his wife gently asks about the pace of spending, as "things we deserve after what this year put us through." A vacation, planned somewhat impulsively, that he frames explicitly as needing to "get away from all of it" — the accident, the case, the year of appointments and paperwork the settlement represented the closing chapter of. Each purchase, taken alone, sounds almost reasonable, even sympathetic. Taken together, they represent a pattern: the money is being spent not according to any financial plan, but according to an unconscious logic of getting rid of it as quickly as possible, as though holding onto it too long would mean continuing to hold onto the accident itself. By the time his shoulder has fully healed as much as it's going to heal, the money that was meant, at least in part, to cushion a future with a permanent limitation is largely gone, and the financial planner conversation from month one never happened at all.

A different case, carrying a distinct emotional charge from the man's accident but landing in the identical spending pattern: a woman receives a settlement following a workplace injury that ended a physical job she'd held for over a decade, compensation intended, at least in part, to bridge her toward retraining for different work. She knows this, explicitly — the structure of the settlement was discussed with her attorney in exactly these terms, a transition fund as much as compensation for what already happened. And yet, instead of allocating any meaningful portion toward that bridge, she spends the first several months of the settlement in a pattern she later describes, with real self-awareness, as “trying to buy back the year the injury took from me” — clothes, outings, small luxuries meant to restore a sense of normalcy and enjoyment that the injury and its long recovery had stripped from her daily life. Each purchase, in the moment, delivers a small, genuine lift, a brief return of a feeling she’d been missing since the injury derailed her routine. But the lift never lasts more than a few days before the next purchase feels necessary to sustain it. By the time she’s ready to seriously think about retraining, a significant portion of the money meant to fund exactly that transition has already gone toward recovering a feeling rather than funding a future, and she’s left facing the actual, practical problem the settlement was meant to solve with meaningfully less to solve it with — a harder version of the exact transition the money was originally sized to make easier.

A third case involves a smaller settlement following a minor dispute with a former landlord over an improperly withheld security deposit — a modest sum, recovered after months of frustrating correspondence and a small-claims filing the tenant nearly abandoned twice out of sheer exhaustion with the process. When the check finally arrives, the relief is less about the dollar amount, which is genuinely small, and more about the vindication of having been right, of the landlord finally being made to admit it. That vindication feeling gets spent almost immediately, on a celebratory dinner and a small purchase the tenant describes, grinning, as "my victory lap" — treating the money less like recovered rent and more like a trophy, disconnected from its actual, mundane origin as simply money that should never have left her account in the first place.

A fourth version involves a family who receives a considerably larger settlement following a prolonged dispute over a home construction defect that caused extensive water damage — years of repairs, temporary housing, and mounting frustration finally resolved through arbitration. Unlike the man's car accident, this settlement carries the specific psychic residue of having been let down by professionals they trusted and paid well, and the money that finally arrives gets treated, in the family's own words, as "getting some of our life back." Rather than funding the remaining structural repairs the settlement was explicitly calculated to cover, a meaningful portion goes toward a family vacation and a series of home upgrades unrelated to the original damage — decisions the parents describe as reclaiming the years the dispute cost them, even as the actual water damage in one section of the house remains only partially addressed a year after the settlement cleared.

A fifth case carries a distinctly different emotional register from the others: a man in his forties receives a settlement following a wrongful termination claim against a former employer, a case he pursued less out of financial need — he found a comparable new job within a few months — than out of a genuine sense of principle, a conviction that what happened to him was wrong and needed to be answered formally rather than simply absorbed and moved past. The settlement, when it finally arrives after over a year of proceedings, carries almost none of the grief or physical pain the other cases in this chapter describe.

What it carries instead is a kind of righteous heat, a feeling he describes to his brother as "finally getting what I was owed," language that frames the money less as compensation for a specific, calculable harm and more as a verdict on his own worth and the injustice of how he was treated. That framing turns out to matter enormously for how the money gets spent. Rather than folding it into his and his wife's existing financial plan — a mortgage refinance they'd been discussing for months — he spends a meaningful portion of it on a single, symbolic purchase: a considerably nicer car than anything he's driven before, bought within three weeks of the check clearing, which he describes, half-joking and half-serious, as "a way of showing them it didn't break me." The car isn't really about transportation. It's a physical, visible answer to an injury that was never physical at all, and it gets purchased with a speed and a lack of comparison-shopping that neither he nor his wife would recognize in any other purchase he's made in fifteen years of marriage.

What's actually happening

Settlement money carries a psychological burden distinct from any other windfall in this book, because unlike a bonus or a gift or even an inheritance, it is explicitly, legally, priced against pain — a number arrived at, often through negotiation, as compensation for something that happened to a person's body, their livelihood, or their sense of safety. That pricing creates a strange psychological artifact: the money becomes, in the recipient's mind, entangled with the injury itself rather than simply becoming money. Spending it doesn't feel like an ordinary financial decision. It feels, often unconsciously, like a way of processing or closing out the event the money represents compensation for.

The psychologist Richard Lazarus's framework of coping, referenced earlier in the context of grief, applies here with a specific twist. Lazarus distinguished between problem-focused coping — actions aimed at addressing the actual source of distress — and emotion-focused coping — actions aimed at managing the feeling of distress itself, sometimes at the expense of addressing the underlying problem. A settlement, ironically, often triggers heavy emotion-focused spending precisely because the money itself represents the closing of the problem-focused chapter — the legal case is resolved, the negotiation is over — which paradoxically frees the recipient to spend the money managing the emotional residue of the ordeal rather than treating it as a resource for their ongoing, practical future. The case is closed. The money remains. And without the ongoing legal process to focus on, the emotional processing of the event has nowhere left to go except into spending decisions that feel, subjectively, like closure.

There's a compounding house money element here too, connecting directly back to this book's core mechanism. Settlement money, like an inheritance, arrives without the felt cost of the recipient's own sustained labor — it arrives as compensation determined by lawyers, insurers, and negotiation, disconnected from any ordinary work the recipient did to earn it. That disconnection triggers the same reduced psychic weight this whole book has been tracking, layered directly on top of the emotion-focused spending Lazarus's framework predicts. The money is coded, simultaneously, as not-quite-real by its windfall origin and as something to be gotten rid of by its association with pain — two separate mechanisms pointing in the identical direction, which explains why settlement money often disappears faster than almost any other category of windfall covered in this book.

There's a further complication specific to settlements that neither Lazarus's coping framework nor the house money effect fully captures on its own: the negotiation process itself often requires the recipient to argue, at length and in detail, for the size of their own suffering — describing pain, loss, and disruption repeatedly to lawyers, adjusters, and sometimes juries, in service of arriving at the largest defensible number. That process can leave a recipient in a strange relationship with the eventual figure, having spent months arguing that their suffering was worth exactly this much, which can make holding onto the money carefully feel, obscurely, like continuing to relitigate the case in private, long after the legal process itself has ended. Spending it quickly can function as a way of finally stepping outside that argument altogether — not because the money isn't needed, but because being finished arguing about the injury starts to matter more than being financially prepared for its consequences.

The small-claims example adds a distinct wrinkle: when a settlement arrives as vindication rather than as compensation for genuine ongoing loss, the money can get recoded a second time, on top of the house money effect, as a symbol of being right rather than as a financial resource at all. Spending it on a celebratory gesture isn't really about the dollar amount at that point — it's a way of externalizing and commemorating a feeling of having been wronged and then vindicated, using the money as a prop for that story rather than evaluating it, plainly, as money. This variant tends to affect smaller settlements disproportionately, since larger ones typically carry enough obvious practical weight — medical bills, lost wages, future needs — to keep at least some portion of the recipient's attention on the money's actual financial function even amid the emotional charge.

One final mechanism is drawn from the broader study of self-perception in psychology. Researchers studying how people come to understand their own attitudes and feelings have found that people frequently infer what they believe or feel by observing their own behavior, rather than the reverse — a person doesn't always spend because they feel a certain way; sometimes the act of spending itself becomes the evidence a person uses to conclude the feeling has resolved. Applied to a settlement, this suggests something uncomfortable: the celebratory purchase, the vacation, the "victory lap," isn't only an expression of relief already felt. It may also function as an attempt to manufacture the sense of closure by acting as though closure has already arrived — spending as a way of telling yourself the story is over, rather than as evidence that it actually is. This is part of why the relief such purchases produce tends to be so short-lived: the purchase was never actually tracking an internal state. It was trying to create one, and manufactured resolution rarely holds up the way genuinely processed resolution does.

The wrongful-termination case sharpens a point only briefly touched on in the small-claims example earlier in this chapter, and it's worth drawing out fully here because it shows the vindication pattern at a scale large enough to do real damage. The psychologist Daryl Bem's self-perception theory, referenced earlier in this chapter in a different context, applies with particular force to settlements driven primarily by principle rather than by physical injury or ongoing loss: when a person pursues a claim mainly to establish that a wrong occurred, the eventual settlement functions, psychologically, less like compensation and more like a verdict, and verdicts invite a very different kind of response than compensation does. Compensation asks, implicitly, "what do you need to recover?" A verdict asks, implicitly, "what does this prove?" — and a purchase made to answer the second question is oriented entirely differently than one made to answer the first. The car wasn't bought to meet a transportation need. It was bought as evidence, submitted to an audience that included his former employer, his brother, and, most of all, himself — proof that the injustice didn't leave a lasting mark, purchased in the specific, urgent register of someone still mid-argument with a wrong that technically concluded months earlier when the settlement was signed. This is a variant worth naming distinctly from the grief-driven and injury-driven versions earlier in the chapter, because the emotional fuel here isn't sorrow or physical pain but a kind of unresolved indignation, and indignation, it turns out, is just as capable of routing a settlement away from its intended financial purpose as grief ever is — sometimes more so, since indignation carries its own built-in justification, a sense of being owed that makes the spending feel not just permissible but almost righteous.

What it costs you

The direct financial cost is often the most consequential of any windfall category, because settlements frequently represent a person's only compensation for a genuine, lasting loss — future earning capacity, a career path closed off by injury, ongoing medical needs — and spending that compensation on short-term emotional relief rather than the long-term needs it was calculated to address leaves the underlying problem the settlement existed to solve still substantially unsolved. The woman whose settlement was meant to bridge her toward retraining now faces that transition with meaningfully fewer resources than the settlement was designed to provide, precisely because the money got spent processing the injury rather than addressing its practical consequences.

The subtler cost is what happens to the emotional processing itself when spending substitutes for it. Purchases made in an attempt to "get back" a feeling an injury or ordeal took away rarely deliver a lasting version of that feeling — the relief is usually temporary, tied to the purchase itself rather than to any genuine resolution of what happened. This means the underlying grief, fear, or loss the spending was trying to manage often remains largely unaddressed even after the money that might have funded genuine practical recovery is gone, leaving a person in the difficult position of having spent both the money and a significant window of time without making durable progress on either the financial or the emotional side of what the settlement represented.

There's a compounding cost specific to families, illustrated by the water-damage example: when a settlement is meant to fund a concrete, verifiable repair — finishing the structural work, replacing what was actually damaged — and instead funds an unrelated celebration, the original problem doesn't just remain unsolved. It often becomes measurably more expensive to solve later, since deferred repairs frequently worsen with time, and the household now has to fund the same fix from a considerably smaller pool of remaining resources, or from future income that was never budgeted to cover it. The settlement, in these cases, doesn't just fail to close the loop it was meant to close. It can leave the household in a genuinely worse position than if the dispute had simply been resolved through direct repair rather than a monetary award at all.

How this shows up without you noticing

Listen for the specific justification language settlement spending tends to produce — "we deserve this after what this year put us through," "I need to get away from all of it," "this is basically free compared to what we've been through." Each of these phrases makes a purchase sound emotionally earned rather than financially evaluated, which is precisely how ordinary discretionary spending discipline gets bypassed. None of these feelings are illegitimate — the underlying difficulty is real. But notice that the phrase is doing double duty: it's expressing something true about the hardship, and it's also quietly exempting the purchase from the scrutiny it would otherwise receive. Catching the phrase is usually enough to catch the pattern.

A second, more structural tell is whether the practical, forward-looking conversation about a settlement ever actually happens versus keeps getting deferred. The man's roof-repair-equivalent conversation — his wife's suggestion of a financial planner — is a useful marker: if that kind of conversation gets agreed to in principle but never scheduled, and weeks pass with only informal, individual spending decisions filling the gap, that drift is itself the pattern operating in real time, not a neutral delay before getting around to it eventually.

The overrides

Separate the closure of the case from the closure of the feeling, explicitly. The legal process ending does not mean the emotional processing is finished, and treating a large purchase as a stand-in for that processing rarely delivers what it's being asked to deliver. If you notice yourself reaching for spending specifically to feel like the ordeal is "over," pause and ask whether what you actually need is a different kind of support — time, rest, a conversation, genuine practical planning — that a purchase is being asked to substitute for.

Name what the money was actually calculated to address, and protect that portion first. Settlements are often composed of distinct components — medical costs, lost income, pain and suffering, future needs — even when they arrive as a single lump sum. Before any discretionary spending, identify what portion of the settlement corresponds to genuine ongoing or future needs, and treat that portion as functionally already spoken for, protected from the emotion-focused spending pattern this chapter describes.

Allow yourself a smaller, consciously bounded portion for genuine relief, decided in advance rather than discovered through spending. There's nothing wrong with using some of a settlement for something that restores a sense of normalcy or enjoyment after a hard stretch — but deciding that amount in advance, deliberately, is a fundamentally different process than discovering it retroactively by noticing, months later, how much has already gone that direction.

Get the financial-planning conversation on the calendar before the money arrives, not after. If a settlement is anticipated, schedule the practical conversation — with a partner, an advisor, or simply yourself with a notepad — for a specific date before the check clears, rather than leaving it as an open-ended "we should talk about this sometime" that easily gets crowded out by weeks of smaller, easier decisions once the money is actually sitting in the account.

Distinguish vindication from compensation when a settlement follows a dispute you clearly won. If part of the appeal of the money is the satisfaction of having been proven right, let yourself enjoy that feeling directly and separately from the money — acknowledge it, sit with it, tell the story to a friend — rather than routing the entire feeling through a purchase. The vindication and the dollars are two different rewards, and only one of them needs to be spent.

If a settlement is imminent, write out what the injury or dispute actually cost you, in full, before the check arrives. Medical bills, missed work, replaced property, ongoing needs — the complete list, not just what the settlement covered. Reading that list back once the money lands is a far more reliable anchor for how to use it than the emotional relief of the case simply being over.

Rule to remember: *money that was priced against your pain is still just money — spending it faster doesn't make the thing that happened to you happen any less. Protect the portion meant for your actual future before you let grief spend the rest.*

Chapter 6 — The Gift

Why Money From Someone Who Loves You Feels Less Like Yours

Her grandmother presses an envelope into her hand at the end of a visit, the way she has every visit since her granddaughter turned eighteen — a check, always a little more than expected, always accompanied by the same instruction: "Don't spend it on anything sensible. Get something you'll actually enjoy." This particular check is larger than usual, a milestone-birthday gift, and it comes with an unusually direct addendum: "I mean it. I don't want to hear you put this toward rent."

Driving home from the visit, she finds herself already narrating the check's future out loud to no one in particular — a kind of running commentary on what she might do with it that has a distinctly different tone than the internal conversation she has with herself about her own paycheck. There's no version of this drive where she considers, even briefly, whether the check might better serve her overdue car maintenance or the credit card balance she's been chipping away at for a year. Her grandmother's instruction has already done its work before the money has even cleared, giving her full permission to skip the deliberation she'd normally apply automatically.

She doesn't put it toward rent. She also doesn't, in any meaningful sense, treat it as money at all in the weeks that follow — it becomes, instead, a kind of permission slip, spent across a handful of purchases she describes, even to herself, as "not real spending" because it's "Grandma's money," money that exists in a category entirely separate from her actual financial life. A significant portion goes to a single splurge — a designer bag she'd never have considered buying with her own earnings — and the rest dissolves across a string of smaller purchases so forgettable she can't reconstruct them a few months later, purchases made with a specific, breezy quality of not-quite-looking at price tags that she never brings to her regular spending. What's notable isn't that she spent a birthday gift on herself; that's precisely what her grandmother asked her to do. What's notable is the specific quality of unreality the money carried the entire time she held it — spent with a looseness she'd never apply to an identical sum from her own paycheck, even though her grandmother's explicit instruction was simply to enjoy it, not to treat it as somehow less financially significant than it was. A year later, she can describe the bag in detail. She can't reconstruct where the rest of the check went, only that it's gone, considerably faster than an equivalent bonus from work would have gone.

A different shape of the same pattern, this one without any explicit "spend it on yourself" instruction attached at all: a young couple receives a substantial cash gift from one set of parents toward a home down payment — generous, given with real love, intended explicitly and specifically for that purpose, discussed in detail at the dinner where the check was handed over. Both sets of parents are proud, a little emotional, and the moment feels significant, almost ceremonial. And yet, in the months before the house purchase actually closes, a meaningful chunk of the gift gets redirected, almost accidentally, toward wedding-adjacent expenses that crept over budget, toward a car repair that "might as well come from the house fund since we'll top it back up later," toward a handful of decisions that individually felt minor and collectively left the down-payment fund several thousand dollars short of where it needed to be. Neither partner ever sits down and decides, consciously, to spend the house money on something else — each individual redirection happens in a moment of minor financial pressure, justified by the thought that it's a temporary borrow from a fund that still technically has plenty in it. When the shortfall becomes undeniable, close enough to the closing date that there's no more time to quietly rebuild it, both partners are visibly surprised — neither can point to a single moment of deciding to spend "the house money" on something else, and yet the money is measurably gone, dissolved through a dozen small, individually reasonable-feeling decisions, each one made easier by the fact that the gift never quite felt like their money in the way their own combined savings did.

A third version, milder in scale but revealing in its own way, shows up at a graduation, where a young man receives cash gifts from several relatives, each individually modest, adding up across the day to a genuinely useful sum for someone just starting out. He describes the collective total, afterward, as "graduation money" — a single, mentally fused category rather than a set of individual gifts from individual people, each of whom might have had a different hope for how it would be used. Within the month, the entire sum is gone, spent on a spontaneous trip with friends to celebrate the milestone, a use that several of the relatives, had they been asked individually, might have gently steered him away from in favor of something that would still exist in a year. He isn't dishonoring anyone's intentions, exactly — none of them specified a use. But the speed and totality of the spending reflects, once again, the same underlying pattern: money that arrived as a gift, however earned the underlying milestone was, gets treated with a permissiveness no equivalent sum from his own part-time earnings would ever receive.

A fourth version shows up in a newly married couple who receive a substantial collection of cash gifts at their wedding, in lieu of the traditional registry, at the explicit request they'd made to their guests. The total is significant — larger than either partner has ever held jointly — and it arrives at a moment already saturated with celebration, gratitude, and a certain giddy sense that ordinary rules are temporarily suspended. In the honeymoon-adjacent weeks that follow, a meaningful portion goes toward upgrades to the honeymoon itself, a round of thank-you gifts more lavish than necessary, and a handful of "starting our life together" purchases for the home that neither partner would have approved from their individual, pre-wedding savings without far more deliberation. Neither partner experiences any of this as reckless in the moment; it all feels like a natural extension of the wedding's celebratory logic. It's only months later, comparing the wedding-gift total against what actually remains, that they recognize how much of a genuinely significant financial head start dissolved into an extended celebration that, while joyful, left little durable trace behind it.

A fifth version shows the pattern operating in a relationship without the built-in generational warmth of a grandmother's birthday check: two close friends in their thirties start a small side project together, and when it's unexpectedly acquired by a slightly larger company for a modest sum, one friend — who contributed meaningfully more capital at the outset — insists on splitting the proceeds evenly anyway, framing the extra share to her friend explicitly as a gift, a way of thanking him for the labor and creative direction he brought even though his initial financial stake was smaller. He's genuinely moved by the gesture, and also genuinely uncomfortable with it in a way he can't quite name at first. In the weeks after the money arrives, he spends his unexpected extra share almost entirely on group experiences — dinners, a weekend trip, small gifts for mutual friends — in a pattern he later realizes was an attempt to distribute the discomfort of the gift outward, to make it feel less like something he alone received and more like something the whole friend group got to share in, as though spreading the money thin enough would dissolve the awkwardness of having been given more than he'd technically earned. None of the individual purchases are unreasonable, but the pattern, once he notices it in hindsight, reveals something the other gift scenarios in this chapter don't quite capture: sometimes gifted money gets spent quickly not because the recipient wants to indulge or because the giver invited indulgence, but because holding onto it in its original, undiluted form feels socially uncomfortable in a way that spending it — especially spending it on shared, visible experiences — quietly resolves.

What's actually happening

Gifted money sits at a strange intersection this book hasn't quite covered yet, because unlike a bonus or a refund, a gift explicitly and openly announces itself as separate from the recipient's own earned resources — there's no ambiguity to untangle, no hidden truth to reveal, as there was with the refund's disguised paycheck. And yet, counterintuitively, that very explicitness seems to deepen the house money effect rather than neutralize it. Money given openly, with love, specifically as a gift rather than as compensation for anything, may be the single most house-money-coded category of windfall in this entire book, precisely because its giver often actively encourages the recipient to treat it as separate, indulgent, exempt from ordinary financial scrutiny — as the grandmother did explicitly, and as countless gift-givers do implicitly, through the simple act of wrapping money in celebration rather than obligation.

A specific psychological layer is at work here, connected to research on the social meaning of money — the idea, studied extensively in behavioral economics and sociology, that money is never purely fungible in practice because it carries social relationships and meanings alongside its numerical value. A gift of money doesn't just transfer purchasing power; it transfers, symbolically, a piece of the relationship between giver and recipient. Spending it "responsibly" — on rent, on debt, on unglamorous obligations — can feel, to the recipient, like a kind of rejection of the gift's actual spirit, a failure to honor the generosity and intention behind it. This creates real pressure, distinct from ordinary house money psychology, toward spending gifted money specifically on enjoyment or indulgence rather than on structural financial priorities, even when the recipient's actual financial situation would benefit far more from the latter.

The down-payment example reveals a second mechanism: gifted money that's earmarked for a specific, large future purpose — a house, a wedding, an education — often gets treated as less protected than money the recipient saved themselves toward the identical goal, because the gift arrived all at once, fully formed, without the recipient's own accumulated discipline reinforcing its importance along the way. Money you save yourself, dollar by dollar across two years, builds a kind of psychological momentum and protectiveness as it grows — you watch it accumulate, you feel what it cost you to build. Money that arrives as a single gift skips that entire process, and skipping it means skipping the protective instinct that process would have built alongside the balance.

There's a further wrinkle specific to gifts that neither settlements nor bonuses carry in quite the same way: the giver is often still present, watching, which creates a strange double pressure. On one hand, as described above, there's pressure to spend the gift in the spirit it was given, particularly when the giver explicitly frames it as indulgent money. On the other hand, there's frequently an unspoken pressure to demonstrate that the gift is being handled "well" — a pressure that can push in the opposite direction, toward performing responsibility rather than actually practicing it. Both pressures point away from the plain, unemotional evaluation the money would get if it had simply arrived as a raise, and navigating between them consciously, rather than defaulting to whichever pressure feels loudest in the moment, is most of what this chapter is asking of you.

The graduation-money example illustrates a further wrinkle: when several gifts arrive together, from several different givers, at a single occasion, they tend to get psychologically pooled into a single undifferentiated category — "graduation money," "wedding money," "birthday money" — that erases the individual intentions of each giver entirely. A grandmother's fifty dollars and an uncle's two hundred dollars, given with potentially very different hopes for how they'd be used, dissolve into one collective sum evaluated as a single windfall event rather than as a set of distinct gifts each carrying its own relationship and its own possible meaning. This pooling effect compounds the house money coding already at work, since a large, pooled, occasion-branded sum reads even more strongly as a windfall than any single contributing gift would have on its own.

A final layer distinguishes gifts from every other windfall category in this book: the relational stakes of getting the response wrong. Unlike a tax refund or a forgotten account, a gift carries an implicit social contract — the giver expects some kind of emotional response, and the recipient often feels pressure to perform gratitude in a specific, visible way. Sociologists studying gift exchange have long observed that gifts are never purely economic transactions; they carry expectations of reciprocity, acknowledgment, and demonstrated appreciation that pure market transactions don't. Spending a gift quickly and visibly — on something the giver can see, hear about, or notice — can function, in part, as a performance of that gratitude, a way of showing the giver their generosity registered and mattered. This isn't cynical or manipulative; it's a genuinely warm impulse. But it does mean gift spending is subject to a social pressure that bonus or refund spending never carries, which is one more reason gifts, of all the categories in this book, resist the plain, unemotional evaluation that would otherwise protect them.

The friends' case reveals a variant of the social-meaning-of-money mechanism on its own terms, since it involves neither a family hierarchy nor a celebratory occasion, the two contexts the earlier examples in this chapter both share. Gift exchange between peers of ostensibly equal standing carries its own particular tension, one sociologists studying reciprocity and equity in relationships have documented directly: a gift that disrupts an assumed baseline of fairness between equals — in this case, an even split despite an uneven initial investment — can produce genuine discomfort in the recipient precisely because it introduces a form of inequality into a relationship that had previously been organized around rough parity. Spending the excess quickly, and spending it specifically on shared, visible experiences rather than on private accumulation, functions as an unconscious attempt to restore the relationship's felt equilibrium — not by returning the money, which would reject the gift outright and risk its own kind of offense, but by converting a private windfall into a shared one, redistributing the discomfort of imbalance back out into the friendship in a form more palatable than a solitary bank balance. This is worth distinguishing clearly from the indulgence-driven spending in the grandmother's-check example: the friend wasn't spending to enjoy himself freely. He was spending, in part, to make an uneven gift feel even again, which is its own distinct motive entirely, and one worth recognizing precisely because it can drive gift money out the door just as quickly as any more familiar form of house-money looseness, while feeling, from the inside, like generosity rather than avoidance.

What it costs you

The direct cost shows up most sharply in exactly the kind of earmarked-but-undefended gift the couple experienced — money given for a specific, meaningful purpose that quietly erodes through small, individually reasonable redirections until the purpose it was meant to serve is measurably harder to achieve. This is a particularly painful version of the windfall pattern, because it isn't just money lost; it's frequently a delay or diminishment of a goal both the giver and the recipient genuinely cared about, undermining the very intention behind the gift.

There's also a relational cost, and it's worth being honest about it. Gift-givers, especially parents and grandparents, often notice, even if they never say so directly, how a gift was ultimately used — and while most genuinely do want their gift enjoyed rather than hoarded, there's frequently a difference between watching a gift contribute to something durable and watching it dissolve without a trace. This isn't a reason to spend a gift joylessly out of obligation to the giver's unstated wishes. It's a reason to spend it consciously, so that whatever choice is made — indulgence or structure or some blend of both — is actually a choice, rather than a default produced by the money's felt unreality.

There's a third cost, subtler still, that shows up specifically in the young woman's recurring pattern with her grandmother's checks. Because each individual gift felt small enough not to matter — one designer bag, one splurge at a time, spread across years — she never once totaled up what the pattern actually added to across the full run of birthdays and holidays it covered. Looked at individually, each gift was exactly what her grandmother intended: a small, guilt-free joy. Looked at in aggregate, across a decade of identical checks treated identically, the pattern represents a meaningful sum that could have funded something considerably larger and more lasting — and the reason it never did isn't that any single decision was wrong, but that no single decision was ever evaluated against the pattern it was part of.

A final cost connects back to the graduation-money pooling effect: when several gifts get treated as one undifferentiated sum, the individual relationships behind them get flattened along with the money itself. A grandmother's gift and an uncle's gift, pooled into an anonymous "party money" total and spent on a single group trip, lose whatever distinct meaning each giver might have hoped their specific contribution would carry. This isn't primarily a financial cost — it's a relational one, a quiet erosion of the individual thoughtfulness behind each gift, replaced by a single undifferentiated windfall that could have come from anyone.

How this shows up without you noticing

The clearest signal is the language of borrowing that appears around earmarked gifts specifically — "we'll top it back up later," "it's basically the same account," "we'll figure out the difference before closing." Each of these phrases treats a specific, purpose-built fund as more flexible than it actually is, precisely because the money inside it never felt as firmly defended as money the recipient saved themselves. If you notice yourself or a partner using this kind of language about a fund with a specific stated purpose, that's the moment worth stopping at — not because a single small redirection is catastrophic, but because the language itself reveals the fund has already stopped being treated as fully off-limits.

A second tell shows up in the phrase "not real spending" or its variants — "this doesn't count," "this is just fun money" — applied to a purchase made with gifted funds. This language performs the exact discount this chapter has been describing, treating a genuine purchase, with genuine opportunity cost, as somehow exempt from the accounting that would apply to the identical purchase made with earned money. If you catch the phrase in your own thinking, that's the signal the gift has already been recoded as less real than it actually is.

The overrides

Honor the gift's spirit without abandoning your own financial judgment. A gift-giver's instruction to "enjoy it" or "don't be responsible with it" reflects real love and real generosity, and it's worth taking seriously — but taking it seriously doesn't require applying zero judgment to how it's spent. You can honor the spirit of celebration a gift carries while still asking the same basic questions you'd ask of any other sum of money: does this purchase actually bring me the enjoyment being offered, or is it simply the easiest way to make the money disappear quickly?

Protect earmarked gifts with the same structural seriousness as earmarked savings. If a gift is given for a specific purpose — a down payment, an education, a major goal — move it, immediately, into whatever structure protects your own saved money for that same goal, so it stops sitting in a general account where it's vulnerable to the dozen small, reasonable-feeling redirections that quietly eroded the couple's house fund. The gift deserves the same defenses your own labor-earned savings get, not fewer.

Decide the split between indulgence and structure consciously, and tell the giver if it feels right to. If a portion of a gift is genuinely meant for enjoyment, decide that portion deliberately and let the rest go toward whatever actually serves you — and if your relationship with the giver allows for it, telling them how you used it, including the structural part, often deepens rather than diminishes the gift's meaning to them.

Watch for the small-borrow pattern on any earmarked fund, and name it the first time it happens. The first time you notice yourself "borrowing" from an earmarked gift for something unrelated, even with every intention of paying it back, treat that as a signal worth taking seriously rather than a harmless one-off — it's usually the first domino in the exact pattern that quietly ate the couple's down payment.

Un-pool multiple small gifts before deciding what to do with the collective total. If several individually modest gifts arrive together at a single occasion, resist the urge to treat the sum as one undifferentiated "party money" category. Consider each gift, briefly, on its own terms — who gave it, what they might have hoped for it — before deciding on a use for the whole. This doesn't require spending each gift separately, only thinking about them separately before pooling them.

If you regularly receive the same kind of gift from the same person, add up the total across the years, once. A recurring birthday check, treated individually, rarely feels worth deep consideration. The same checks added across a decade often reveal a genuinely significant sum — worth knowing, if only so any future installments in the pattern get evaluated with that larger total in mind rather than treated, each time, as a small, forgettable extra.

Rule to remember: *a gift given in love doesn't need to be spent carelessly to be honored — the person who gave it to you almost certainly wants it to genuinely help you, and structure is one of the ways money actually helps.*

Chapter 7 — The Equity Payout

Why a Life-Changing Sum Can Vanish Into a Life You Didn't Choose

He'd worked at the company for four years when the acquisition closed, and the number that hit his account afterward was larger than every paycheck he'd ever earned there, combined, several times over — the kind of sum that changes the shape of a conversation with a financial planner from theoretical to immediate. For the first few weeks, he does very little with it, stunned into a kind of paralysis, checking the balance the way you'd check on something you don't quite believe is real. He tells a few close friends, carefully, watching their reactions, half expecting someone to point out that this can't actually be real, that some administrative error is about to reverse itself. No one does. The number stays. Then, gradually, the paralysis gives way to something else: a sense that a sum this large means the ordinary rules of careful spending simply don't apply to him anymore in the way they used to.

Two years later, a considerable portion of it is gone — not through any single catastrophic decision, but through an accumulation of choices that each, individually, felt proportionate to his new reality. A significantly larger apartment, in a significantly more expensive part of the city, justified by the thought that he could obviously afford it now. A car he'd never have seriously considered a year earlier. A habit of picking up the check for friend groups, generous in a way that felt good and also quietly established an expectation he now feels obligated to maintain, one that's grown, without any single conversation about it, into a fairly reliable pattern every time the group goes out. Investments in two friends' business ventures, made with a casualness — minimal due diligence, decisions reached over a single dinner conversation, numbers he never actually verified independently — that he would never have applied to money he'd saved slowly himself, because some part of him still isn't treating this money as fully, seriously his, even two years and a considerably smaller remaining balance later. When a financial planner he finally does consult, well over a year after the acquisition closed, walks him through what remains against what arrived, he's visibly startled by the gap — not devastated, the sum remaining is still meaningful, but startled in the specific way of someone confronting a number that doesn't match the story he'd been telling himself about how carefully he'd been living.

A parallel case, different scale, same shape: a woman who receives a meaningful but more modest equity payout — not life-changing in the way the acquisition was for the man above, but still, by a wide margin, the largest single sum of money she's ever held — finds herself, in the months after, gradually adjusting her everyday spending upward in ways she doesn't fully register as connected to the payout at all. Restaurants she wouldn't have chosen before. A gym membership at a considerably pricier studio, joined on something close to a whim after a friend mentioned it. Small, frequent upgrades that don't individually register as "spending the payout" because they don't feel connected to that specific sum in her mind — they feel like her new, ordinary life, which is precisely the trap. Eighteen months later, a friend asks, in passing, what she ended up doing with the payout, and she genuinely struggles to answer — there's no single purchase or investment she can point to, no clean story, just a gradually elevated cost of living that has, by now, become invisible to her, absorbed so completely into "normal" that she no longer experiences any of it as connected to a windfall at all. The payout didn't just fund a handful of purchases. It quietly reset what felt normal, and the new normal is now sustained by her regular income in a way the payout itself never actually justified long-term.

A third case involves a couple who receive a joint windfall through stock options that vested at an unusually favorable time, a sum large enough to pay off their mortgage outright several times over. Rather than an immediate spending spree, their version of the pattern is slower and more structural: they don't pay off the mortgage, or invest the sum seriously, or make any single large decision at all for nearly two years, largely because the size of the number makes every decision feel simultaneously too important to rush and too abstract to fully engage with. In the meantime, they gradually adopt a pattern of "small treats" — nicer everyday purchases, more frequent dining out, upgraded everyday conveniences — funded not from the payout directly but from their regular income, on the reasoning that the payout sitting untouched in the background makes their regular spending feel lower-stakes than it used to, even though the payout itself is never actually touched to cover any of it. The money doesn't get spent. Its mere presence changes their relationship to money that isn't the payout at all — a variation on the hedonic reset that doesn't require the windfall to be liquidated to still quietly loosen the household's everyday discipline.

A fourth case, smaller in scale but instructive in its own right, involves an early employee at a startup that's acquired for a modest sum relative to the man's four-year windfall — enough to comfortably cover a year of expenses, but nowhere near retirement-changing money. Because the payout is modest enough to feel almost like "a really good bonus" rather than a genuinely transformative sum, she never applies the caution either the man or the couple eventually reach for, precisely because the size never triggers the sense of gravity that would prompt seeking outside advice. She treats it, from the outset, as spending money for an ambitious home renovation and a round of travel, reasoning that a sum this size doesn't warrant the same seriousness a truly life-changing payout would. Eighteen months later, the money is gone and her financial position is, in practical terms, identical to where it was before the payout arrived — a reminder that the house money effect doesn't require an extraordinary sum to fully activate, only a sum that feels, relative to a person's usual financial life, sufficiently disconnected from ordinary effort.

A fifth case shows the pattern at the junior end of the scale, where the payout is smaller than any other example in this chapter but the underlying psychology runs almost identically: a woman two years into her first job out of college has a portion of her restricted stock vest during an unexpected run-up in her company's share price, netting her, after taxes, an amount equal to roughly four months of her salary — a genuinely meaningful sum for someone her age and tenure, though nowhere near the scale of the other payouts in this chapter. She has almost no prior experience managing a sum this size, and unlike her more senior colleagues, she has no established investment account, no relationship with a financial advisor, and no real framework for what to do with a number that large beyond a vague sense that she should probably "do something smart with it." In the absence of any clear plan, the money sits in her checking account for a few weeks, visible every time she checks her balance, until a friend suggests a spontaneous international trip to celebrate both the vest and an upcoming milestone birthday. She says yes almost immediately, books a considerably more expensive version of the trip than she would have from her regular savings, and returns to find that nearly sixty percent of the vest is gone, spent not through any single decision that felt reckless but through an extended, celebratory stretch that felt, the entire time, like an appropriate way to mark a genuinely exciting career milestone. She doesn't regret the trip. What she notices, months later, comparing notes with a colleague who diverted a similar vest almost entirely into an index fund, is that she never actually considered the alternative — the money arrived pre-coded, by virtue of its sheer unfamiliarity and the excitement of the milestone it represented, as an occasion to be marked rather than a resource to be allocated, and no one at any point suggested to her that those were two different, separately decidable questions.

What's actually happening

Large equity payouts combine two mechanisms this book has already named separately, and the combination is more potent than either alone. First, the house money effect operates at unusually high intensity here, because the sheer size of the sum relative to the recipient's prior financial life makes it feel almost abstractly unreal — a number too large to metabolize as ordinary, spendable money, which paradoxically makes it easier, not harder, to spend carelessly, since carelessness with an abstraction feels lower-stakes than carelessness with something concretely understood.

Second, and more consequentially for the woman in the second example, this is where hedonic adaptation enters the picture directly — the well-documented psychological finding that people adjust rapidly to improved circumstances and recalibrate their sense of "normal" around the new baseline, a process researchers have studied extensively in the psychology of well-being. A large payout doesn't just provide spending money; it resets the recipient's reference point for what an ordinary lifestyle costs, and once that reset happens, ongoing spending at the new, elevated baseline no longer registers, subjectively, as spending the payout at all — it registers as simply living, normally, in the new life the payout established. This is precisely why the woman's restaurant choices and gym membership don't feel connected to the payout in her mind: the payout has already done its damage by resetting what "normal" means, and the ongoing spending at that new normal is now sustained by her regular paycheck, invisibly propped up by a windfall that's no longer even part of the conscious accounting.

The man's casual investments in friends' ventures reveal a third layer, connected to research on risk tolerance following gains, the same territory Thaler and Johnson's original house money studies covered directly. A sum large enough to feel abstractly unreal doesn't just get spent more loosely — it gets risked more loosely, with less due diligence, less caution, precisely the pattern Thaler observed at the blackjack table scaled up to a magnitude most casino gamblers never approach. The size of the payout, far from producing more caution, produced less, because the psychic distance between "money I earned through years of steady work" and "money that appeared because a company got acquired" is, for many recipients, enormous — larger, if anything, than the psychic distance most people feel toward a modest bonus or refund.

The woman's case adds a final piece, and it's the piece that makes equity payouts uniquely dangerous compared to every other category in this book: the invisibility of the hedonic reset once it's fully absorbed. A truck or a watch or a renovation, once purchased, remains visible — a concrete thing a person can point to and connect back to the windfall that funded it. A gradually elevated cost of living leaves no such marker. There's no single receipt to examine, no specific purchase to regret or defend, just a slowly shifted baseline that, eighteen months out, has become simply "how much things cost now," indistinguishable in the recipient's own mind from ordinary inflation or ordinary life changes. This is precisely why she couldn't answer her friend's question. The money wasn't spent in any way she could narrate. It was absorbed, structurally, into her sense of what normal costs — the single hardest version of this pattern to catch, because by the time it's fully set in, it no longer looks like spending at all.

The couple's untouched-payout case reveals yet another variant worth naming, because it demonstrates that a large sum doesn't need to be spent to loosen behavior — its mere existence in the background can do the work. This connects to research on wealth effects in consumer spending, the broader finding that people spend differently when they perceive themselves as wealthier, even when the specific wealth in question is illiquid, untouched, or entirely unrelated to the transaction at hand. A rising home value or an untouched investment account can measurably shift everyday spending behavior even though no part of that wealth has actually been converted to cash, and a large, dormant equity payout appears to function the same way: its presence recalibrates a household's felt sense of their own financial cushion, which loosens everyday discretion, without the payout itself ever needing to be liquidated or directly spent at all.

A final dimension connects to temporal discounting — the well-established finding in behavioral economics that people systematically value a dollar available today more highly than an equivalent dollar available in the future, discounting future value at a rate that often exceeds what any rational, patient calculation would justify. A large equity payout, precisely because it's so much bigger than anything the recipient has managed before, can trigger an unusually steep version of this discounting: the future uses of the money — a fully secured retirement, a paid-off home, a genuinely resilient financial position decades out — feel abstract and distant, while the present pleasures available right now feel vivid and immediate. The size of the payout, rather than making the future feel more secure, can paradoxically make the present feel more urgent to enjoy, because a sum that large finally makes certain present indulgences feel achievable for the first time, and that achievability itself becomes difficult to defer.

The junior employee's case isolates a variable the other examples in this chapter don't fully separate out: the difference between a payout arriving into an existing financial infrastructure — a brokerage relationship, an established habit of allocating windfalls, a financial advisor already in the picture — versus one arriving into a genuine vacuum. Her more senior colleague's near-automatic decision to route a similar vest into an index fund wasn't necessarily evidence of superior discipline; it likely reflected years of prior exposure to the mechanics of what to do with unexpected liquidity, infrastructure the junior employee simply hadn't had time to build yet. Where infrastructure is absent, the mind doesn't default to caution — it defaults to the nearest available frame for what a large, unexpected sum is "for," and in the absence of any competing frame, an exciting personal milestone happening to coincide with the payout is often the frame that wins by default, not because it's the most rational use of the money but because it's the only frame actively presenting itself in the moment. This points to a practical asymmetry worth naming: younger, less financially experienced recipients of equity payouts are, in some respects, more vulnerable to this chapter's pattern than older, more established ones, precisely because they haven't yet had the years of exposure needed to build the kind of automatic, protective infrastructure that makes routing a windfall toward a considered purpose feel like the obvious first move rather than one option among several equally available ones.

What it costs you

The direct cost, at this scale, is often the largest in dollar terms of any category in this book, simply because equity payouts frequently represent sums an order of magnitude larger than a bonus or a refund — which means the same percentage lost to house-money spending represents an enormous absolute amount, often the difference between a payout that could have fundamentally altered someone's financial trajectory for decades and a payout that instead funded a few years of an elevated lifestyle before quietly fading into the background of an income that can no longer sustain it on its own.

The subtler and, in some ways, more dangerous cost is the hedonic reset itself. Once a lifestyle has recalibrated upward around a windfall's temporary presence, reversing that recalibration is genuinely difficult — not because the person lacks discipline, but because the new baseline no longer feels like an indulgence to give up; it feels like a reduction in ordinary life, a step backward, even though it was never actually sustainable on ordinary income to begin with. The woman didn't choose, at any single moment, to permanently commit to a pricier gym and pricier restaurants funded by her regular salary. The payout made that choice for her, gradually, by moving the goalposts before she ever consciously decided to move them.

There's a further cost specific to the early-employee example: a modest payout that never triggers the sense of gravity a life-changing sum would produces a particularly insidious version of this pattern, because the recipient never consults anyone, never seeks a second opinion, and never applies the scrutiny that a genuinely transformative number would have prompted almost automatically. The absence of drama around the payout becomes, paradoxically, the very thing that lets it disappear without the safeguards a larger, more alarming number would have earned. Modest windfalls may in fact carry more risk in aggregate than dramatic ones, precisely because they slip past the internal alarm systems that larger, more obviously consequential sums would trigger.

How this shows up without you noticing

Because this pattern rarely announces itself through a single traceable purchase, the tell is almost always a vague, hard-to-source sense that your everyday spending has quietly shifted — restaurants you wouldn't have picked before, upgrades that feel unremarkable rather than notable, a general sense of "this is just what things cost now" applied to categories that used to prompt at least a moment's hesitation. If you find yourself unable to explain, when asked directly, exactly what a large payout was used for, that inability to answer is itself diagnostic. The money that gets spent in a single traceable purchase is easy to reckon with later. The money that gets absorbed into an elevated baseline rarely gets reckoned with at all, precisely because it no longer looks like spending by the time anyone thinks to ask.

A second, related tell is a general resistance to comparing prices or shopping around for things you used to compare carefully. If a windfall has recently landed, notice whether your threshold for "worth comparing" has quietly risen — whether purchases that once prompted a quick search for a better price now simply get made, without the friction that used to be a routine part of your decision process.

The overrides

Deliberately delay any lifestyle change until the payout has been treated as a resource, not an identity shift. Before making any change to your ongoing, recurring cost of living — housing, memberships, standing habits — separate a large payout mentally from your regular income entirely, and ask whether your regular income alone would justify the change. If it wouldn't, the change is being funded by the payout, whether or not it feels that way, and it deserves to be recognized as a payout-funded decision rather than absorbed silently into "normal life."

Apply your normal due-diligence standard to any windfall-funded risk, regardless of how abstract the sum feels. If a payout is large enough to feel unreal, that feeling is precisely the signal to apply more scrutiny to any investment or risk-taking with it, not less. Treat every dollar of it as though it were the hardest-earned dollar you've ever had, and let that standard — not the payout's abstract size — govern how carefully you evaluate any risk you take with it.

Build a floor under your new baseline before you let it become permanent. If a lifestyle shift genuinely reflects a considered, deliberate choice rather than a hedonic drift, make sure it's actually sustainable on your ongoing income, independent of the payout, before treating it as your new normal — and if it isn't, decide consciously whether the payout is meant to fund a temporary season of elevated living or a permanent shift, rather than discovering the answer by accident when the payout runs out.

Schedule a periodic outsider's review of where the payout actually went. Because this pattern is uniquely invisible — absorbed into "normal life" rather than tied to specific purchases — a standing check-in every several months, with a partner, a friend, or an advisor who can ask plainly "where did it go and where is the rest of it," catches the drift long before it fully disappears into an unrecoverable new baseline.

Apply the same seriousness to a modest payout as you would to a life-changing one. Don't let the relative size of a payout determine how carefully you treat it — a sum that feels merely "nice" rather than transformative is just as capable of disappearing without a trace, and the absence of obvious gravity is often exactly what allows the pattern to run unchecked in cases that seem too modest to warrant real caution.

If this is your first experience with a payout of this size, borrow someone else's infrastructure before building your own from scratch. If you don't yet have an established habit, account structure, or advisor relationship for handling unexpected liquidity, don't let the payout itself be the first thing that fills that vacuum. Ask a colleague further along in their career what structure they use, or spend a single afternoon setting up the basic accounts and rules you'll want in place before the money arrives, so the payout has somewhere considered to land instead of defaulting to whatever occasion happens to be nearby when it does.

If a payout is anticipated, write down your current cost of living, in detail, before it arrives. A dated, specific snapshot of what your life actually costs today is the single most useful tool for noticing a hedonic reset later, since the reset is otherwise nearly impossible to detect from inside it. Revisit the snapshot every six months or so and compare honestly.

Rule to remember: *a large sum feeling abstract is exactly when it needs the most scrutiny, not the least — the size of the number should raise your caution, not lower it, and your new normal should be able to survive without it.*

Chapter 8 — The Forgotten Account

Why Money You'd Written Off Disappears Twice

An email arrives from a state unclaimed-property office, the kind of message that looks enough like spam that she almost deletes it unread. It isn't spam. It's notice of a small brokerage account, opened by an employer eleven years earlier during a job she barely remembers, abandoned when she changed companies and never rolled it over, sitting untouched and accumulating modest interest in a database she didn't know existed until this exact email. She spends a confused ten minutes trying to remember the job well enough to believe the notice is legitimate before she calls the number listed, half expecting to be told it's a scam. It isn't. The amount, once she completes the claim process, is a genuine surprise — not life-changing, but real, several thousand dollars she had, in every meaningful sense, already mentally written off as gone, spent, irrelevant to her current financial life.

The money clears into her account on a Thursday. By the following Thursday, roughly a third of it is already spent — a spontaneous concert ticket for a show she wouldn't normally have splurged on, a dinner out that turned into a considerably more expensive night than planned, a small home purchase she'd been putting off. Each purchase arrives with a specific internal narration: this doesn't count the same way, because a week ago this money didn't exist in my life at all. None of these purchases feel connected, in her mind, to any actual financial plan. They feel like play money, precisely because the money had already died once in her accounting — she'd stopped counting it as hers years earlier, which means its return doesn't register as "gaining money I have," it registers as a kind of bonus round, money existing entirely outside her real financial life even after it's sitting, quite concretely, inside her real bank account. A friend, hearing the story a few months later, asks the obvious question — what did you end up doing with the rest of it — and she has to think for an uncomfortably long moment before admitting she isn't entirely sure.

A smaller-scale version of the identical pattern: a man finds an old envelope while cleaning out a late relative's garage, containing several hundred dollars in cash that had clearly been tucked away and forgotten decades earlier, the bills themselves a slightly different design than the currency in circulation now, a small physical reminder of just how long this money has been sitting outside anyone's active accounting. He never considers, even briefly, adding it to his regular savings or using it toward any bill. The money gets spent within the week, on a whim, on things he later can't fully list, and he describes the whole episode to a friend with a kind of amused shrug: "It was just found money, so." That phrase — just found money — does an enormous amount of psychological work in a single sentence, and it's worth noticing how automatically it gets reached for, as though found money exists under different physical laws than money that arrived through any other channel. His friend, hearing the phrase, doesn't question it either — the framing is so culturally familiar, so instantly accepted by anyone who hears it, that neither of them pauses to notice how strange it actually is to treat a legal, spendable sum of cash as somehow less real simply because of how it turned up.

A third version shows up in a couple who, while switching banks, discover a small dormant checking account neither of them remembers opening, left over from a brief period years earlier when they'd tried a short-lived budgeting system involving multiple separate accounts. The balance is modest but not trivial, sitting untouched long enough to raise a genuine question about how it was overlooked for so long. Rather than folding it back into their current accounts and treating it as part of their existing financial picture, they instead treat the discovery itself as an occasion — "we should do something with this since we found it" — and within a few weeks it's gone toward a home item neither had planned to buy, justified explicitly by its status as a surprise rather than evaluated on whether it was actually the best use of that sum given their other, ongoing financial goals.

A fourth version, and perhaps the most easily overlooked of all, involves a woman who receives a notice that a class-action settlement she'd forgotten she was even eligible for — related to a minor product issue years earlier — has resulted in a modest check being mailed to her automatically. She has no memory of filing any claim, no memory of the product issue itself, and initially assumes the letter is a scam before confirming it's genuine. Because the money arrives entirely without any active effort or even conscious awareness on her part — she didn't search for it, didn't request it, didn't do anything to earn its arrival beyond having once purchased an ordinary product — it registers as close to pure, unattached luck as any windfall in this book, and it's cashed and spent within days on an impulse purchase she describes to her partner, laughing, as "money that fell out of the sky."

A fifth, quieter version shows up in an older man who, while finally sorting through decades of paperwork after retirement, discovers a small, long-dormant pension credit from a job he held briefly in his twenties — a genuinely tiny sum in the context of his overall retirement savings, worth barely a few hundred dollars once processed. He's mildly amused by the discovery more than anything, and the money, once it arrives, gets folded without any real deliberation into a spontaneous outing with his grandchildren, a purchase he later describes with real fondness but can't quite connect, even in memory, to the specific pension credit that funded it. The smallness of the sum here is the point: even a windfall too modest to register as a meaningful financial event still gets filtered through the same zero-reference-point mechanism, spent with a looseness disproportionate to its size purely because of how completely it had been forgotten.

A sixth version shows the pattern operating inside a small business rather than a personal account: the owner of a two-person design studio, reconciling the books at year-end with her accountant, discovers a client overpayment from nearly three years earlier that was never refunded or applied to any invoice — a clerical oversight that sat quietly in the business's operating account the entire time, effectively hiding in plain sight inside a balance she checked regularly but never audited closely enough to notice the discrepancy. The amount is meaningful relative to the studio's typical monthly revenue, and her accountant's first question is practical: which client, and should it be returned. It shouldn't — the statute for the client to claim it has long since passed, and the accountant confirms the funds are legitimately the studio's to keep. What happens next is telling: rather than folding the discovered sum into the business's regular operating reserves, where it would function exactly like the rest of the studio's working capital, the owner mentally earmarks it as a kind of bonus to herself, separate from the business's real finances, and within a month has used a meaningful portion of it to fund a conference trip and a round of new equipment upgrades that hadn't been part of the studio's actual capital planning for the year. She never applies to this money the same scrutiny she applies to every other dollar that moves through the business — the multiple approval steps, the comparison shopping, the deliberate weighing of whether a purchase serves the studio's actual priorities for the year — because the money never registered, psychologically, as part of the studio's real finances at all. It registered as a discovery, and discoveries, as earlier examples in this chapter have shown, come with their own unwritten permission to be treated more loosely than money that was always counted.

What's actually happening

Forgotten and found money represents, in a sense, the house money effect in its most concentrated and unguarded form, because unlike every other category in this book, this money was never even present in the recipient's ongoing mental account of their own resources. A bonus, a refund, even an inheritance — all of these existed, at minimum, as something the recipient knew was coming, even briefly. Forgotten money skips that step entirely. It was already zero in the recipient's mental ledger, meaning its return doesn't feel like an addition to an existing total — it feels like a pure, unattached gain, arriving from outside the recipient's financial life altogether rather than as part of it.

This connects to a foundational finding from Kahneman and Tversky's work on framing effects: how a gain or loss is presented relative to a reference point determines how it's experienced, independent of its objective size. For money the recipient had already fully written off, the reference point is zero — not their actual account balance including this asset, but their felt sense of their own resources, which had long since excluded it. Against a reference point of zero, any recovered amount reads purely as gain, with none of the loss-aversion protectiveness that would apply to money already counted as part of an existing total. This is precisely why forgotten money gets spent with even less resistance than a bonus or a gift: those categories, at minimum, get briefly incorporated into the recipient's sense of their total resources before spending begins. Forgotten money often skips incorporation entirely, moving straight from "doesn't exist" to "spent" without ever passing through a phase where it was genuinely counted as part of the recipient's real financial picture.

There's a phrase worth examining directly here, because it appears constantly in exactly this context and reveals the mechanism cleanly: "found money." The phrase itself performs the psychological work of exempting the sum from ordinary financial scrutiny before a single dollar has been spent — money that is "found" is implicitly framed as belonging to a different category of ownership than money that is earned, saved, or even given, as though discovery itself confers a kind of temporary, lesser claim on the funds. It doesn't. Once money is legally and practically yours, the manner of its arrival has no bearing whatsoever on what it's actually worth or what it can actually do for you — but the phrase "found money" makes that fact very easy to forget in the moment it matters most.

The friend's unquestioning acceptance of the phrase points to something worth naming about this category specifically:

found money is, culturally, one of the few kinds of windfall that comes with near-universal social permission attached. Nobody raises an eyebrow at "I found some old cash and blew it on a nice dinner" the way they might at "I inherited money and spent it in a month." The social script is already written, already agreed upon by everyone involved in the conversation, which means there's essentially no external friction slowing the spending down — no raised eyebrow, no gentle pushback, nothing to interrupt the pattern except the recipient's own awareness of what's actually happening.

The dormant-checking-account example points to a final layer worth naming: the occasion of discovery itself can function as a kind of manufactured celebration, similar to the ceremonial framing that sometimes surrounds a gift. Finding forgotten money produces a small burst of surprise and pleasure that has nothing to do with the sum's actual size, and that burst seems to demand, psychologically, some kind of matching action — spending it, marking the occasion, doing something with it that honors the surprise. This is worth distinguishing clearly from the money's actual financial merit: the feeling of discovery is real and pleasant, but it's a feeling about the moment of finding, not a fact about what the smartest use of the money actually is, and conflating the two is exactly what leads a rediscovered account to fund a home item that was never actually the household's top financial priority.

The class-action example adds a final, subtle dimension: money that arrives with genuinely zero active effort on the recipient's part — not even the effort of searching an unclaimed-property database, just an envelope showing up unbidden — represents perhaps the purest test case for the zero-reference-point mechanism in this entire book. There was no anticipation to build a mental placeholder for this money, no memory of the underlying claim to connect it to, nothing at all standing between the money's total absence from the recipient's awareness one day and its presence in her account the next. The speed and totality of the spending that followed isn't a character flaw specific to this one recipient. It's close to the cleanest possible demonstration of what happens when a reference point sits at true zero and a dollar amount, however modest, appears against it with no felt history attached at all.

The design studio owner's case demonstrates that the zero-reference-point mechanism described above operates just as cleanly inside a business's mental accounting as it does inside a personal one, which is worth noting explicitly since business owners often assume, incorrectly, that the more formal, deliberate nature of business finances offers some inherent protection against this book's patterns. It doesn't. A business's operating account is, in principle, subject to exactly the same rigorous evaluation for every dollar that moves through it — that's the entire premise of careful bookkeeping — but a discovered sum that was never part of the account's known, budgeted total slips outside that rigor in precisely the way personal forgotten money slips outside a household's regular scrutiny. The studio owner didn't lower her standards for the business generally; she simply never applied those standards to this specific sum, because the sum had already been filed, before a single dollar was spent, into a mental category — "found," "extra," "extra to me personally" — that sat outside the business's ordinary accounting altogether, despite technically being business revenue subject to exactly the same priorities as every other dollar the studio earns.

What it costs you

The direct cost is often modest in any single instance — forgotten accounts and found cash tend to be smaller sums than inheritances or equity payouts — but the pattern itself is instructive precisely because of how cleanly it reveals the mechanism at its most extreme. If money that was already, unambiguously, legally the recipient's own can vanish this quickly purely because it was briefly forgotten, it demonstrates just how little the actual, objective facts of ownership matter to how carefully a windfall gets defended. The psychological category the money gets filed under does almost all of the work, regardless of the money's legal or financial reality.

The subtler cost is the missed opportunity these small windfalls represent in aggregate. Forgotten accounts, uncashed checks, unclaimed property, security deposits never followed up on — collectively, these represent a meaningful pool of money most people will encounter at least once or twice across a lifetime, money that arrives with genuinely no attachment, no complicated emotional weight, no source tag connected to a person or an ordeal. That lack of complication makes this category, in principle, the easiest windfall in this entire book to allocate thoughtfully — there's no grief to process, no relationship to honor, no injury to grieve. And yet it's spent with some of the least resistance of any category, precisely because "just found money" provides such an effective, ready-made excuse to skip the thinking altogether.

A final cost applies more broadly than it might first appear: many people never even go looking for this category of money in the first place, precisely because it requires a kind of active curiosity — checking unclaimed-property databases, tracking down old accounts, following up on deposits — that feels disproportionate to the payoff when the money has already been mentally written off as gone. The habit of writing off money too early doesn't just affect what happens after it's found. It affects whether it ever gets looked for at all, which means the true cost of this pattern includes not just the money spent carelessly once recovered, but a second, invisible pool of money that never gets recovered in the first place because no one thought it was worth the trouble of looking.

There's a compounding version of this cost specific to households that experience the discovery-as-occasion pattern more than once. Because each individual rediscovery feels like an isolated, celebratory event rather than part of a recurring pattern, households rarely notice how often it happens across a lifetime — an old account here, an unclaimed refund there, a forgotten deposit somewhere else — each one triggering the identical spend-it-quickly response without ever being recognized as one recurring behavior worth addressing at the level of the pattern rather than the individual instance.

How this shows up without you noticing

Listen for the phrase "just found money" in your own mouth or in a friend's story, and treat it as a flag rather than a punchline the moment you hear it. The phrase is doing real psychological work every time it's used, quietly exempting whatever sum follows it from the scrutiny that would apply to any other dollar in your life. The other reliable tell is the speed of the spending relative to the size of the discovery — money that gets spent within days of being found, with no consideration given to any competing use, is a near-certain sign the zero-reference-point effect is running unchecked.

A third tell is treating the discovery itself as an occasion requiring some kind of matching celebratory action, rather than simply folding the money into your existing accounts as though it had always been there. If the first instinct on finding forgotten money is "we should do something with this" rather than "this is now part of what we have," that instinct is the mechanism announcing itself.

The overrides

Run it through the zero-reference-point check directly. The moment you notice yourself thinking "it's just found money," pause and translate the sentence back into its accurate form: this money is now part of my actual financial life, exactly as real as anything else in my account. The fact that you'd forgotten it existed says something about your memory, not about the money's worth.

Treat rediscovered money as though it had arrived through an ordinary raise. Ask the same question this book has returned to repeatedly: if this exact sum had shown up as a modest, permanent bump in my regular income instead of as a single rediscovered lump sum, what would I actually do with it? That question strips away the "found" framing and reconnects the money to the same financial seriousness you'd apply to any other resource.

Use the lack of complication as an asset, deliberately. Because found and forgotten money rarely carries grief, obligation, or a source tag, it's uniquely well suited to serving a clear, unemotional financial purpose — a debt payoff, a genuine emergency fund contribution, a goal that's been stalled for lack of funding. Precisely because there's no emotional pull toward any particular use, this is a good category of windfall to route, quickly and deliberately, toward whatever your financial plan actually needs most, before an easy default fills the vacuum instead.

Resist the social script instead of accepting it automatically. The next time someone tells you a "just found money" story, or you catch yourself about to tell one, treat the phrase as a flag rather than a punchline. You don't need to lecture anyone about it, but declining to apply the same casual exemption to your own found money, quietly, is enough to change how the money actually gets used.

Actually go looking for money you may have written off too early. Periodically check unclaimed-property registries, old employer retirement accounts, security deposits from past residences, and similar sources most people never think to revisit. The habit of looking is worth building independent of any specific expected payoff, since the true cost of this pattern includes money that never gets found at all because no one thought to search.

When forgotten money surfaces, deposit it and wait a full week before deciding anything. The urge to mark the occasion with a purchase is strongest in the first hours after discovery. A week of simply letting the money sit, fully counted as part of your real balance, is usually enough for the celebratory impulse to fade and an ordinary, considered evaluation to take its place.

Rule to remember: *money doesn't stop being yours just because you forgot about it — and the fact that it's easy to spend without a second thought is exactly why it deserves a* *second thought.*

Chapter 9 — The Lucky Win

Why One Stroke of Luck Can Make Your Whole Financial Life Feel Like House Money

He wins four hundred dollars on a scratch-off ticket bought on a whim at a gas station, a genuinely rare stroke of luck for someone who buys maybe two or three tickets a year, mostly as an idle habit rather than any real gambling pattern. The win itself is small in the context of his overall finances — not remotely life-changing, a pleasant surprise rather than a windfall in the scale this book has mostly been discussing. He texts a photo of the ticket to his brother with a laughing emoji, buys himself something small on the way home to celebrate, and mostly forgets about it within a few days, the way anyone would forget a genuinely minor win.

What happens over the following weeks is more interesting than the win itself: he finds himself, repeatedly, a little looser with money generally, in ways that have nothing directly to do with the four hundred dollars, which was spent within days on nothing memorable. He picks up a round of drinks he normally wouldn't have offered to buy. He upgrades a takeout order without really registering the decision. He says yes, with unusual ease, to a slightly pricier plan for an upcoming friend's birthday that he'd normally have gently pushed back on. He feels, in some diffuse, hard-to-articulate way, like his month has extra room in it — a feeling that traces back, if you follow it carefully, to a four-hundred-dollar scratch-off win that's long since been spent and has no actual bearing whatsoever on his regular monthly budget. When his card gets declined at a gas pump three weeks later — an embarrassing, entirely avoidable overdraft — he's genuinely confused for a moment about how his account got so tight, before slowly reconstructing, purchase by small purchase, a month that had been quietly running looser than any month before it, without a single decision that, on its own, looked like the cause.

A related but distinct version, this one without any gambling involved at all: a woman has an unusually good month trading a small amount of money in a personal investment account she treats as separate, deliberately, from her core savings — a modest amount she's designated specifically for this kind of higher-risk experimentation, walled off intentionally from the rest of her financial life precisely so that any losses there can't threaten anything essential. The month goes well, considerably better than she expected, and she feels, understandably, a real surge of pride and competence, a sense that she's gotten good at something difficult. In the weeks that follow, she notices herself extending a version of that same looseness to decisions entirely unrelated to the investment account — approving a larger home purchase than she'd normally consider, feeling less resistant than usual to an impulse buy, generally operating with a subtly elevated sense of how much financial room she has, even though the actual gain, while real, represents a genuinely small fraction of her total financial picture and has no logical bearing on decisions in completely separate parts of her life. It's only when a friend, mid-conversation, asks whether the home purchase decision had anything to do with her good trading month that she stops and actually traces the connection for the first time, mildly startled to realize her friend is right — the two things had felt, until that exact moment, completely unrelated.

A third example closes the loop on how ordinary this pattern really is: a man wins a modest raffle prize at a community event

— a gift card, not cash, worth a genuinely small amount — and finds himself, that same weekend, agreeing to an unplanned dinner out that costs several times the value of the prize itself, waving off his own usual instinct to suggest cooking at home instead. He never connects the raffle win to the dinner decision at all, not even in hindsight, because the prize itself was never spent on the dinner — it wasn't cash, it wasn't fungible with the meal in any direct way. And yet the mood the win produced clearly traveled with him into a decision the prize had no logical connection to whatsoever, the smallest and cleanest illustration in this book of how little the actual dollar amount of a win matters to the size of its psychological aftershock.

A fourth version, and perhaps the most relatable of all, involves a woman who receives an unusually glowing performance review at work — no bonus attached, no raise mentioned yet, purely verbal praise from a manager she respects. She leaves the meeting genuinely elated, and on the drive home stops at a store she wouldn't normally browse and leaves with a purchase she hadn't planned on, one she later describes as "celebrating the review." Nothing about the review itself put a single additional dollar in her account. The purchase was funded entirely by her regular checking balance, exactly as available and exactly as limited as it was that morning before the meeting. What changed wasn't her financial position. It was her mood, and her mood, for one afternoon, borrowed the looseness this whole book has been tracking and applied it to an entirely ordinary shopping trip that had nothing to do with any actual windfall at all.

A fifth example pushes this chapter's mechanism to its most surprising edge yet: a man attends a friend's engagement party where the friend announces, with real excitement, an unexpected work bonus that's funding a significant upgrade to the wedding they're now planning. Nothing about this news changes the man's own financial position in any way whatsoever — he receives no money, no gift, no windfall of his own, only the secondhand experience of watching someone close to him receive one. And yet, driving home from the party, he stops at a store he wouldn't normally visit on a weeknight and makes an impulse purchase he later can't fully explain, describing the mood afterward as something like "caught up in the excitement of the night." Nothing about his own account balance changed between leaving for the party and making the purchase. What changed was his proximity to someone else's good fortune, absorbed secondhand through the shared celebratory atmosphere of the evening, in a way that produced a real, measurable loosening of his own spending caution despite having no logical connection to his own finances at all.

What's actually happening

This chapter closes the book by returning directly to the scene that opened Chapter 1 — the blackjack table — and showing how the same mechanism operates even when the "win" in question is small, disconnected from any ongoing gambling behavior, or entirely unrelated to the domain where the looseness eventually shows up. This is, in some ways, the most important chapter in the book precisely because it reveals that the house money effect isn't confined to the specific windfall itself. It can bleed outward, coloring a person's general sense of financial safety and looseness well beyond the boundaries of the actual lucky event, in a way none of the other, more contained chapters fully capture on their own.

Thaler and Johnson's original research on the house money effect documented exactly this kind of spillover: subjects who experienced a prior gain showed increased risk tolerance not just with the specific winnings from that gain, but in subsequent, ostensibly separate decisions, suggesting the effect operates less like a strict accounting rule confined to a specific pool of money and more like a temporary shift in overall psychological state — a kind of financial mood, elevated by a recent win, that colors judgment across a wider range of decisions than the win itself would rationally justify. The man's four hundred dollars didn't just get spent loosely. It left behind a residue of looseness that outlived the money itself by weeks, coloring decisions that had nothing to do with the original win.

A related concept comes from the psychologist Robert Zajonc's research on affect and cognition, which established that emotional states generated by one experience can influence judgments in a completely unrelated domain, often without the person consciously connecting the two — a phenomenon sometimes described as affect infusion. A person in a good mood generally makes more optimistic estimates and takes on more risk across unrelated decisions than the identical person in a neutral mood, even when the good mood has no logical bearing on the decision at hand. A lucky win produces exactly this kind of generalized positive affect, and that affect infuses judgment well beyond the specific dollars involved — which is precisely why the woman's successful trading month showed up in an unrelated home purchase decision, and why the man's gas-station win showed up in takeout orders that had nothing to do with scratch-off tickets.

This is the mechanism this entire book has been circling from Chapter 1 onward, now visible in its most concentrated and, in a sense, most honest form: money doesn't need to be a formal windfall category — an inheritance, a bonus, a settlement — to trigger this pattern. Any experience of unearned or lucky gain, however small, however disconnected from a person's core financial life, can produce a temporary state of loosened judgment that outlasts the money itself and colors decisions the original win never touched.

The gas-pump moment and the friend's offhand question, taken together, point to the same underlying truth from two different angles: this pattern operates almost entirely below the level of conscious narration. Neither the man nor the woman set out to spend their whole month differently because of a small win. Neither would have predicted, in advance, that a scratch-off ticket or a good trading month would touch decisions about takeout orders or home purchases. The mood infusion Zajonc's research describes doesn't announce itself. It just quietly recolors the background against which every other decision that week or month gets made, and the only way to catch it is to go looking for it deliberately, because it will never announce itself on its own.

The raffle-prize example demonstrates the outer edge of this mechanism, worth naming explicitly as this book's final piece of research grounding: the mood infusion doesn't require the win to be liquid, spendable, or even directly connected to the decision it eventually touches. A gift card, a modest prize, a piece of good news entirely disconnected from money — any of these can trigger the same generalized positive affect Zajonc's research describes, and that affect can bleed into a financial decision made hours or days later with no logical thread connecting the two beyond the shared, ordinary experience of a good mood. This is, in the end, the most important reframe this book offers: house money was never really about the money at all. It was always about the mood the money's arrival produces, and the mood is the actual variable worth learning to notice — because the mood will keep showing up, in ever-new disguises, long after any single windfall this book has named has been spent, forgotten, or folded quietly into an ordinary life.

It's worth stepping back, in this final chapter, to notice how neatly this mechanism closes the loop that opened the book at the blackjack table. The man playing looser with his winnings wasn't experiencing a phenomenon specific to gambling — he was experiencing the most visible, most easily observed version of a mood-driven looseness that operates identically across every other chapter in this book, just usually with less obvious triggers and less obvious consequences. The inheritance, the bonus, the refund, the settlement, the gift, the payout, the forgotten account — each one produces its own version of the mood this chapter has finally named directly. What differs across chapters is the story attached to the money's arrival.

What doesn't differ is the underlying shift in felt safety and looseness that story produces, every time, regardless of how large, small, expected, or surprising the windfall actually was.

The engagement-party case extends this chapter's mechanism into territory worth naming explicitly as the book's final and most surprising finding: the mood infusion Zajonc's research describes doesn't require the win to be your own. Emotional contagion — the well-documented tendency for moods to transfer between people in close proximity, particularly in group settings charged with celebration or excitement — means that witnessing someone else's windfall can produce a genuine, measurable version of the same affective state a personal win would produce, even though nothing about the observer's own financial position has changed in the slightest. The man at the engagement party didn't misunderstand whose bonus was being celebrated; he knew, perfectly well, that the money was his friend's and not his own. But the mood the announcement produced didn't respect that boundary, because mood, as this chapter has shown throughout, was never really about the money in the first place — it's a contagious state that spreads through proximity and shared experience, entirely indifferent to whose account balance actually changed. This is, in a real sense, the outer boundary of everything this book has been describing: if a stroke of someone else's luck, absorbed secondhand at a party, can measurably loosen a bystander's own spending discipline, then the house money effect isn't only a story about what happens to money you receive. It's a story about a mood that money — yours, someone else's, real or merely nearby — is unusually good at producing, and that mood will keep finding its way into your decisions from angles no chapter in this book could fully anticipate.

What it costs you

The direct cost of any single lucky win is usually small, by definition — these are rarely the largest windfalls in a person's life. But the diffuse looseness a lucky win produces can quietly inflate spending across weeks or months in ways that are almost impossible to trace back to their actual source, which makes this pattern uniquely difficult to catch and correct compared to every other chapter in this book. A bonus or an inheritance at least announces itself as the thing being spent. The mood residue from a lucky win rarely announces itself as anything at all — it just feels, subjectively, like a good month, right up until the actual numbers reveal it wasn't.

The deeper cost is what this reveals about financial judgment generally: if a modest, unrelated stroke of luck can measurably shift how carefully a person guards money in a completely separate part of their life, it suggests financial discipline is considerably less stable, moment to moment, than most people assume it to be. This isn't a discouraging finding — it's a genuinely useful one, because it means the discipline most people believe is a fixed personal trait is, in fact, a state that fluctuates with mood, recent events, and unrelated strokes of luck, which means it can be actively protected and stabilized rather than simply hoped for.

As this book closes its final chapter, one compounding cost deserves attention: a string of small, unremarkable lucky wins across a year — a modest bonus here, a small refund there, a good month, a scratch-off ticket, a rediscovered account — can produce a nearly continuous low-level mood infusion if a person never learns to name the pattern, meaning the looseness never fully resets between windfalls the way it might if each one were recognized and consciously contained. For someone who happens to encounter several of the categories in this book across the same year, the effects can stack in ways that are easy to miss precisely because no single event feels large enough to explain the whole picture. This is, in the end, the deepest reason this book exists: not because any one windfall is dangerous in isolation, but because the same unnamed mechanism runs quietly beneath all of them, and naming it once means you can catch it every time it shows up again, in whatever form it takes next.

How this shows up without you noticing

The clearest tell for this chapter's pattern is the disconnect between what triggered your looseness and what your looseness is actually spent on. If you notice yourself saying yes more easily than usual to a purchase that has no logical relationship to a recent win — a raffle prize funding an unrelated dinner, a good trading month funding an unrelated home decision — that disconnect is the entire signature of affect infusion. The mood doesn't announce which decisions it's touching. It just makes everything feel slightly more affordable for a while, and the only way to catch it is to ask, deliberately, whenever a larger-than-usual decision follows closely on the heels of good news: would I be making this call if the good news hadn't happened?

A second, cumulative tell worth watching for across a full year rather than a single week: if you notice a general sense of financial ease that doesn't seem to track your actual account balances — a persistent feeling of "things are fine" that outpaces what your numbers would justify if you actually looked closely — that gap between felt ease and verified reality is often the accumulated residue of several small, forgotten wins compounding quietly in the background.

The overrides

Notice the mood, not just the money, after any win. After any lucky gain, however small, check in specifically on your general sense of financial looseness over the following days and weeks — not just how you're spending the winnings themselves, but how you're approaching completely unrelated financial decisions. Naming the mood as a mood, rather than mistaking it for an accurate read on your actual financial position, is the entire intervention.

Contain the win physically, and let the containment do the psychological work. Where practical, keep genuinely lucky, unearned gains in a separate space from your regular spending accounts, even briefly, rather than letting them merge immediately into your general balance where their looseness can spread invisibly into unrelated decisions. The containment isn't about restricting what you eventually do with the money — it's about preventing the mood infusion this chapter describes from bleeding into decisions the win never actually funded.

Run a specific gut check before any decision made shortly after a win, lucky or otherwise. If you're about to make a meaningfully larger financial decision than usual within a few weeks of any stroke of good luck — a win, a great month, an unexpected gain of any kind — pause and ask directly: would I be making this exact decision if the recent win hadn't happened? If the honest answer is no, that's the affect infusion this chapter describes, operating in real time, and naming it is usually enough to at least slow the decision down to where it can be evaluated on its own actual merits.

Ask someone close to you to flag the pattern, since you're the least likely person to catch it yourself. Because this mechanism operates below conscious narration, an outside observer — a partner, a close friend — is often better positioned to notice "you've seemed a little looser with money since that win" than you are. Give that observation real weight rather than dismissing it, since dismissing it is exactly what the mood itself would prefer you do.

Extend the check to non-cash wins as well as cash ones. A raffle prize, a piece of good news, a compliment, a stroke of professional luck — none of these need to be liquid or financial in nature to trigger the same generalized mood shift. Widen your awareness beyond strictly monetary windfalls to any recent positive event that might be quietly coloring a financial decision you're about to make.

Before closing this book, do one last thing: think back across the eight windfalls this book named and ask which

one is most likely to happen to you next. Not which one already has — which one is coming. Write it down, and write down, in advance, the one override from that chapter you're most likely to actually use. Deciding this now, with a clear head, is worth more than anything you'll be able to decide in the moment the money actually arrives.

Rule to remember: *a good month doesn't make the rest of your financial life safer than it actually is — check your judgment as carefully after good luck as you would after bad, because luck changes your mood a great deal faster than it changes your actual numbers.*

Before You Go

There's a version of this book that could have ended differently — a version that told you windfalls are dangerous, that unearned money is somehow lesser, that the only virtuous dollar is a hard-won one. That would have been a simpler, more moralized argument, and it also would have been wrong, and worth explicitly disowning before you close these pages. Nothing in the eight chapters behind you is an argument against receiving an inheritance, enjoying a bonus, celebrating a settlement, accepting a gift, or feeling grateful for a stroke of luck. Windfalls are not a moral hazard. They are simply money that arrived through a different door than the one your paycheck usually walks through — and the only thing that door changes is how carefully your mind, left unchecked, decides to guard what came through it.

That's the entire argument this book has been making, chapter after chapter, windfall after windfall: not that unearned money is bad, but that your relationship to it is quietly, systematically different from your relationship to earned money, in a way you likely never consciously chose and probably never noticed happening in real time. A dollar from an inheritance spends exactly the same as a dollar from a paycheck at the register. It buys the same groceries, pays down the same debt, funds the same future. The only place the two dollars differ is inside your own head, in the split-second calculus that decides how much scrutiny each one deserves before it's gone — and that calculus, as chapter after chapter has shown, quietly favors the windfall every single time, regardless of how large it is, how it arrived, or how careful you otherwise are with money.

If you take away only one thing from this book, let it be the felt sense of that gap — the difference between how you'd treat ten thousand dollars you built over a year of ordinary paychecks and how you'd treat ten thousand dollars that landed in a single check from a lawyer, an employer, a government agency, or a beloved relative. That gap is not a fact about the money. It never was. It's a fact about you, about the particular way your mind is built to sort resources by the story of their arrival rather than by their actual, objective worth — and once you can feel that gap clearly, actually feel it, the way you'd feel a hand on your shoulder, you have something most people never get: the ability to notice the moment it's happening, rather than only reconstructing it in hindsight, eighteen months later, wondering where the money went.

You will have more windfalls in your life. That's a near-certainty, not a maybe — a tax refund most years, very possibly a bonus at some point, quite likely a gift or an inheritance somewhere down the road, and, if you're fortunate, maybe an equity payout or a genuine stroke of luck along the way. None of the chapters in this book were written to prepare you for one specific event and then become irrelevant. They were written to give you a mechanism you can carry forward and apply to whatever form of unearned money shows up next, including forms this book never got around to naming — a lawsuit you never anticipated, a family business sold decades from now, a form of luck that doesn't exist yet. The specific windfall will differ. The house money effect underneath it will not.

Look back, briefly, at the range this book actually covered. Grief money that gets spent trying to hold onto someone, or trying to prove something to them. Reward money that gets mentally split into a responsible half and a permission-slip half. Your own wages, returned to you months late, treated as though the government handed you a gift. Money priced against your own pain, spent trying to outrun the pain rather than address what it left behind. Love, handed to you in an envelope, discounted the moment it arrived precisely because of the affection it carried. A number too large to feel real, quietly resetting what your ordinary life is allowed to cost. Money you'd already stopped counting, returning from nowhere and vanishing just as fast. And a mood, triggered by nothing more than a stroke of luck, coloring decisions that had nothing to do with the luck itself. Eight different doors. One mechanism walking through all of them.

It's worth being honest, one more time, about what this book cannot do. It cannot make the felt lightness of windfall money disappear — that lightness is likely a permanent feature of how your mind works, not a bug you can patch out through reading. Even after finishing every chapter here, the next unexpected check that lands in your account will probably still feel a little unreal, a little like it belongs to someone else, at least for the first few days. What changes, if this book has done its job, is not the initial feeling. It's what happens in the gap right after that feeling arrives — whether you notice it, name it, and let it settle before acting, or whether it runs the whole show uninterrupted the way it likely has every time before now. That gap, stretched wide enough to fit one honest question inside it, is the entire difference between a windfall that quietly disappears and a windfall that actually changes something.

One last thought, and then these pages are yours to put into practice. Somewhere in your life — maybe soon, maybe years from now — you'll be the one standing in the kitchen holding a letter, or staring at a deposit notification, or turning a scratch-off ticket over in your hand, feeling that specific, disorienting lightness this whole book has been describing. When that moment comes, you won't need to remember every chapter, every study, every carefully drawn distinction. You'll only need to remember one thing, the sentence this whole book has been building toward from its first page: *this money doesn't know how it got to me, and it doesn't get to decide, on its own, how carelessly I treat it.* Say that sentence, mean it, and let it buy you the four or five seconds of clear thought that everything else in this book was written to protect. That's not a large ask. It is, in the end, almost the entire difference between a windfall you remember and one you can't quite account for.

Notes & Further Reading

Introduction and Chapter 1 — The House Money Effect. The house money effect is drawn from the work of behavioral economist Richard H. Thaler, whose research across several decades — including his collaboration with Eric J. Johnson on gambling behavior and risk-taking following prior gains and losses — established that people become measurably more willing to take risks with money they perceive as recent winnings than with money from an untethered source, even when the sums are objectively identical. Thaler's broader concept of mental accounting, the finding that people sort money into separate psychological categories governed by different implicit rules rather than treating it as a single fungible resource, underlies the reasoning throughout this book; Thaler was awarded the Nobel Memorial Prize in Economic Sciences in 2017 in substantial part for this body of work. The concept of psychic cost — the subjective, felt weight of effort behind an acquisition, distinct from objective market value — draws on the broader behavioral-economics literature on effort and valuation. The reference-point mechanism described in Chapter

1 draws on the prospect theory developed by psychologists Daniel Kahneman and Amos Tversky, whose foundational 1979 paper established that people evaluate outcomes relative to a reference point rather than in absolute terms, and that losses are experienced as more psychologically painful than equivalently sized gains are pleasurable — a finding sometimes referred to as loss aversion. Kahneman was awarded the Nobel Memorial Prize in Economic Sciences in 2002 for this and related work (Tversky, who died in 1996, was ineligible under the prize's rules).

Chapter 2 — The Inheritance. The distinction between problem-focused and emotion-focused coping is drawn from the work of psychologist Richard S. Lazarus, particularly his collaborative work with Susan Folkman on stress, appraisal, and coping, which established these two broad coping categories as central to how people respond to major life stressors including grief and loss. The concept of a "source tag" persisting on inherited or gifted money reflects observations in the literature on mental accounting and the psychology of inheritance and bequests, an area of ongoing study within behavioral economics and family-wealth research.

Chapter 3 — The Bonus. This chapter extends Thaler's mental accounting framework, cited above, to compensation structured as lump-sum bonuses and distributions, and draws on research into hedonic framing — how the language and delivery format surrounding a financial gain shapes the scrutiny applied to spending it — a subfield connected to prospect theory and to the broader mental accounting literature.

Chapter 4 — The Refund. The flypaper effect in household spending, describing the tendency of money to be spent according to the implicit rules of the mental category it arrives in rather than pooled rationally with other income, is a well-documented finding in public finance and behavioral economics, studied extensively in the specific context of tax refunds and other windfall income by researchers examining consumption responses to fiscal transfers.

Chapter 5 — The Settlement. This chapter returns to Lazarus and Folkman's coping framework, cited above under Chapter 2, applying the problem-focused/emotion-focused distinction to the specific psychological position created when a legal or insurance process concludes and leaves a lump-sum payment in its place.

Chapter 6 — The Gift. This chapter draws on the broader sociological and behavioral-economics literature on the social meaning of money — the observation, developed across work in economic sociology, that money is never purely fungible in lived experience because it carries relational and symbolic meaning alongside its numerical value, a tradition that includes Viviana Zelizer's influential work on the social construction of money's meaning within households and relationships.

Chapter 7 — The Equity Payout. Hedonic adaptation, sometimes called the "hedonic treadmill," is a well-established finding in the psychology of subjective well-being, describing how quickly people adjust to positive changes in circumstance and return toward a relatively stable baseline of life satisfaction; the concept has been studied extensively across decades of well-being research. This chapter combines that finding with Thaler and Johnson's house money research, cited above, to describe how large payouts both fund immediate spending and permanently shift a recipient's baseline expectations.

Chapter 8 — The Forgotten Account. This chapter applies Kahneman and Tversky's reference-point framework, cited above under Chapter 1, to the specific case of money a recipient had already mentally excluded from their felt sense of their own resources, arguing that a zero reference point removes the loss-aversion protectiveness that would ordinarily apply to a recognized asset.

Chapter 9 — The Lucky Win. The concept of affect infusion — the finding that emotional states generated by one experience can influence judgment in unrelated domains, often without conscious awareness of the connection — draws on the work of social psychologist Robert B. Zajonc on the relationship between affect and cognition, and on the broader affect-infusion literature developed in subsequent social-psychology research examining mood's effects on judgment and risk-taking.

Additional concepts referenced across chapters. Moral licensing, referenced in Chapter 3, describes the finding across behavioral economics and social psychology that a virtuous or disciplined act in one domain can create a subjective sense of permission to behave less carefully in a separate, logically unrelated domain — a pattern studied across contexts including consumer spending, ethical behavior, and health choices. Affective forecasting, referenced in Chapter 2, is the study of how accurately people predict their own future emotional reactions to events and purchases; the field, associated with psychologists including Daniel Gilbert and Timothy Wilson, has repeatedly found that people are prone to systematic errors in predicting both the intensity and duration of emotional responses, including the relief expected from a purchase made during emotional distress. Anchoring, referenced in Chapter 4, is among the original heuristics-and-biases findings from Kahneman and Tversky's research program, describing how an initial reference number — even an arbitrary or informally estimated one — measurably influences subsequent judgments and decisions. Wealth effects in consumer spending, referenced in Chapter 7, describe the finding in household-finance and macroeconomic research that perceived changes in wealth, including illiquid or unrealized wealth such as home equity or investment account balances, measurably influence everyday consumption behavior even without any of that wealth being directly spent.

On dual-process reasoning, referenced in Chapter 4. The distinction between explicit, statable knowledge and the automatic, largely unconscious processing that governs much of everyday judgment and behavior is a central theme across dual-process theories of cognition, a body of work that includes but extends well beyond Kahneman's own writing on the subject; Kahneman's *Thinking, Fast and Slow* offers an accessible synthesis of this broader research tradition, describing the interplay between fast, automatic judgment and slower, deliberate reasoning in terms directly relevant to why intellectual understanding of a bias frequently fails to neutralize the bias in the moment it operates.

On self-perception theory, referenced in Chapter 5. Self-perception theory, developed by the psychologist Daryl Bem beginning in the late 1960s, proposes that people often infer their own attitudes and internal states by observing their own behavior, particularly in situations where internal cues are weak or ambiguous — a reversal of the more intuitive assumption that behavior simply follows from a pre-existing internal state. The theory has been extensively studied and applied across social psychology in the decades since, including in research examining how people interpret the meaning of their own consumption and spending choices.

On commitment devices, referenced in Chapter 3. The study of commitment devices — mechanisms that bind future behavior in advance, precisely because willpower and memory alone are unreliable enforcers of a plan once circumstances change — is a well-established area within behavioral economics, with research consistently finding that structural commitment, such as automatically moving money somewhere less accessible, produces materially better follow-through than purely intentional or verbal commitments to a plan.

On emotional contagion, referenced in Chapter 9. The transfer of mood and affective state between individuals in proximity, particularly within group settings, has been studied extensively in social psychology under the heading of emotional contagion, a literature that documents how emotional states can spread between people through shared expression, tone, and context, often below the threshold of conscious awareness on the part of either the person expressing the emotion or the person catching it.

On financial socialization and scale calibration, referenced in Chapter 2. The broader study of financial socialization — how people develop financial habits, judgment, and calibration for handling money at various scales, typically through repeated exposure across childhood and early adulthood — is an active area of research within both psychology and household-finance economics, and offers useful context for why unfamiliar sums, particularly early in a person's financial life, tend to receive less rigorous evaluation than sums closer to a person's established experience.

A note on how to use this book alongside professional guidance: nothing in these chapters is a substitute for advice from a qualified financial planner, tax professional, or attorney, particularly for the larger windfall categories covered in Chapters 2, 5, and 7, where the dollar amounts and legal complexity involved can materially benefit from individualized, credentialed guidance this book was never designed to provide.

What this book offers instead is a way of understanding the psychological terrain a windfall arrives into, so that whatever professional guidance you do seek gets evaluated with a clearer head than the windfall's arrival would otherwise leave you with.

Every named researcher, study, and finding above reflects real, published work in behavioral economics and psychology. Scenarios and individuals described throughout the chapters are illustrative composites, not case studies of specific real people, and are not attributed to any named research.

About This Book

The Windfall Instinct is part of the Money Instinct library, a series of short, focused books each examining one specific way ordinary psychology quietly shapes financial behavior — not through a lack of discipline or knowledge, but through mental mechanisms operating well below the level of conscious decision-making. Each book in the series isolates a single pattern cleanly enough to be genuinely useful: recognizable in your own life, explained through real research rather than invented authority, and paired with concrete ways to interrupt it.

This is not a book of investment advice, product recommendations, or step-by-step financial planning. It doesn't tell you which account to open or what percentage to save. What it offers instead is narrower and, hopefully, more durable: a clear enough understanding of one specific mental pattern that you can recognize it the next time it's operating on you, in whatever form your next windfall happens to take.

If this book was useful, the rest of the Money Instinct library covers other patterns worth knowing — the way earned income quietly expands to fill whatever room a raise creates, the way secrecy around money compounds quietly inside a relationship, the way underearning gets rationalized as humility, the way shame protects a fragile self-image from an honest look at your own numbers, the way panic distorts decisions during genuine financial stress, and the way an invisible ceiling keeps otherwise capable people from ever asking for what they're worth. Each book takes the same approach this one did: a real, named psychological mechanism, shown through close, recognizable scenes rather than abstractions, paired with overrides that live in your own judgment rather than in any specific product or platform.

The library exists on a simple premise: most financial advice targets the wrong layer of the problem. It assumes the gap between what people know and what people do is a knowledge gap, solvable with a better spreadsheet or a clearer rule. Often, it isn't. The gap is frequently psychological — a mechanism running beneath conscious awareness, doing its work regardless of how much the person consciously knows about compound interest or emergency funds. You can know, with total clarity, that a windfall is exactly as real as earned income, and still feel it as lighter in the hand the moment it arrives. Closing that gap between knowing and feeling isn't a matter of more information. It's a matter of naming the mechanism clearly enough that you can catch it operating in real time, which is the entire task this book, and this library, sets out to do.

If a specific chapter in this book landed hardest for you, that's worth paying attention to — not as a verdict on your character, but as useful information about which door your own next windfall is most likely to walk through. Keep that chapter in mind. The next unexpected check, deposit, or envelope that arrives in your life will very likely test exactly the mechanism that chapter described, and having already seen the pattern named and explained once is most of what it takes to catch it the second time.

Also in the Series

Every book in The Money Instinct library stands on its own — read them in any order. If this one was useful, the library continues:

The Money Instinct

The Secrecy Instinct

The Underearning Instinct

The Shame Instinct

The Panic Instinct

The Merge Instinct

The Ceiling Instinct

The Control Instinct

The Legacy Instinct

The Comparison Instinct

The Enabling Instinct

The Austerity Instinct

The Paralysis Instinct

The Retirement Instinct

The Divorce Instinct

The Enough Instinct

The Overconfidence Instinct

The Vigilance Instinct

The Generosity Instinct